Making Connections

Enhance Your Listening Comprehension in Chinese

Simplified Character Edition

Madeline K. Spring

Cheng & Tsui Company
Boston • Worcester

2002 Printing

Published by

Cheng & Tsui Company
25 West Street
Boston, MA 02111-1213 USA
Fax (617) 426-3669
www.cheng-tsui.com
"Bringing Asia to the World"™

Printed in the U.S.A.

Simplified Character Edition
ISBN 0-88727-366-1

TABLE OF CONTENTS

ACKNOWLEDGMENTS

Many people have been involved with various aspects of this project—no one could have imagined its complexity when we began our work a number of years ago.

I deeply appreciate the contributions of the speakers whose voices form the texts for the lessons. Recording "spontaneous" conversations in the cramped confines of a sound studio and making them sound authentic is truly an art, and I have been fortunate to work with such talented people, who accomplished this so gracefully. Most of these men and women are or were graduate students at the University of Colorado, Boulder. They include Wang Wei, Wang Ping, Shelley Wing Chan, Haning Hughes, Liu Yingnan, Zhang Dongming, Zhang Huicong, Wang Yanning, Wang Fengtao, Lu Xiaoyin, Rebecca Li, Liu Changli, and Zhang Huijie. Additionally, I want to acknowledge the able assistance of David Slayton and the other students at the University of Colorado, Boulder, who offered their editorial feedback and made many improvements on the text. Special thanks also to Shelley Wing Chan, Howard Y.F. Choy, Kong Mei, and Shen Ning for their valuable input at various stages of this project.

I am especially grateful to Sandy Adler, Foreign Language Communications Support Specialist for the College of Arts and Sciences at the University of Colorado, for her dedicated assistance with this project. Her time-consuming and painstaking attention to detail made this book possible in its final form. I want to thank Richard Borkowski for help with the first set of recordings, and I especially want to extend my great appreciation to Brett Mann, Sound Engineer at the University of Colorado, who worked patiently for the past year, recording and producing the final version of the audio recordings. Thanks also to Dave Underwood, Manager of Media Design at the University of Colorado, for designing the book cover.

I would like to thank Jill Cheng for her interest in and support of this project. Sandra Korinchak, Production Manager at Cheng & Tsui, has patiently worked to improve the book, and I am very appreciative of her efforts. Thanks also to Alice Shin-yi Kao for her editorial suggestions and work on preparing the index. I also want to express my gratitude to Cheng & Tsui for allowing me to use some artwork from the textbooks *Adventures in Japanese* and *Integrated Chinese*.

Lastly I'd like to acknowledge my daughter Eléna Spring English, who in addition to giving great moral support, made many useful suggestions on graphics, artwork, and the formatting of the text.

I believe this book will help fill a gap in instructional resources for Chinese. Teachers and students can tailor this book to fit their needs, and I am eager to hear feedback about their experiences and about ways the book can be improved.

INTRODUCTION

To the Teacher

Welcome to *Making Connections: Enhance Your Listening Comprehension in Chinese.* This text offers an exciting way for students in beginning and intermediate level Chinese courses to develop and improve aural comprehension skills. The need for an innovative textbook in Chinese that focuses primarily on listening comprehension, and that is flexible enough so it can be implemented directly into various curricula, is keen. The main objective of *Making Connections* is to equip students with listening strategies that will improve their comprehension of naturally-spoken Chinese. These strategies will allow them to communicate much more effectively in Chinese.

Making Connections is *not* intended to function as a main textbook. Grammar explanations are given sparingly, and there is little emphasis on reading. It is assumed that students will gain adequate exposure to work in these areas through their primary textbooks. A minimum of preparation is required for the instructor, and the lessons can easily be assigned to complement regular course materials.

Making Connections is flexible enough to accommodate the needs of a variety of learners and instructors. It can be used as a supplement to a first-, second-, or third- year college course. It is equally effective for students working independently. Even advanced students and heritage learners who are already familiar with the vocabulary used in the conversations in this text will be surprised how much they will learn from working with audiotexts that model the ways idiomatic expressions and other vocabulary items are actually used.

One of the chief complaints of teachers and students of Mandarin is that students are inadequately prepared for "real" Chinese. This situation is common to all students of foreign languages and is perfectly understandable, given that it is important for learners to gain a firm foundation in the basic principles of a language before they are exposed to individual deviations. For this reason it is advisable that students wait to begin work with *Making Connections* until after they have had a basic introduction to the study of Chinese (at least the equivalent of one semester at the college level). At this point they will be prepared to handle listening tasks that are more challenging.

Sometimes listening comprehension gets overlooked in Chinese courses. Research has shown that students can only create in the language after they have been presented with sufficient meaningful input. *Making Connections* provides this input in a conversational format that engages students' interest.

Before students can use new vocabulary and grammatical patterns in meaningful ways, it is important that they are exposed to natural speech that occurs in normal conversation. When comprehension skills are taught systematically, students are better equipped to cope with linguistic situations that may be slightly beyond their level. As confidence in dealing with these situations builds, students will be willing to take greater risks in producing their own language, and their attitude toward learning the language will be even more positive. The strategies learned in improving listening comprehension will readily transfer into reading comprehension and other aspects of language learning.

The conversations in this text are presented in authentic and naturally-paced language, and the lessons are constructed to support students' existing knowledge and develop mastery of new vocabulary, grammatical patterns, and sociocultural formalities in ways that are compatible with genuine communication. The activities emphasize vocabulary and structures that naturally occur in real conversations between native speakers of Mandarin. Vocabulary and grammar become tools for the student to use Chinese actively, rather than discrete items that are meant to be pieced together like a jigsaw puzzle. Minimal grammatical explanations are given when appropriate, and the linguistic activities have embedded grammatical goals. These activities, like those mentioned above, are consistently contextualized according to the topic of the lesson. This approach complements, reinforces, and in some cases previews material that students have been or will be taught more systematically in their main textbooks or by their instructors. Instructors need not worry that students cannot grasp every word of the dialogues or that some of the vocabulary will seem too advanced for students at earlier levels of language proficiency. *Making Connections* is intentionally challenging and sometimes even ambiguous (as is the language learning process itself!). Please avoid the temptation to transcribe the dialogues for your students or to ask them to do this. Invariably there may be one or two students who will force themselves to master every single utterance they hear. But our goal is to train students to learn listening skills so they can catch what is being said at a normal pace by speakers who are not making accommodations for the linguistic level of their audience. The use of *realia* (newspaper advertisements, receipts, medical prescriptions, etc.) adds by exposing students to small bits of authentic Chinese writing at early stages of their language acquisition process. Keep in mind that the tasks that involve these authentic texts are generally quite simple—in fact, the most important part of these exercises is for students to see what "real Chinese" looks like.

For this reason, too, teachers should be tolerant of instances in which the speakers on the tapes make grammatical or pronunciation "mistakes" or say things in ways that are different from textbook Chinese or from the way any one individual might say something. Even though each of the speakers is a native speaker of Mandarin, inevitably s/he will say things in ways that are not perfectly "correct." As teachers we need not fear that this will have a negative impact on our students—it is simply a fact that language usage varies widely, and it is imperative that students come to grips with this concept early on. Given the dramatic impact of international travel, study abroad, and the widespread reliance on media and Internet, it is increasingly more difficult to categorize specific usage as belonging to any one region. When appropriate, terms or pronunciations that are generally associated with speakers from PRC or Taiwan have been provided. These distinctions offer instructors an opportunity to point out these differences whenever relevant to curriculum or approach. Similarly, photos and realia from both PRC and Taiwan allow students to see variety in Mandarin-speaking environments. In these ways *Making Connections* helps bridge the gap students will encounter as they make the transition from the classroom environment to more realistic situations.

Your students' ability to work with the audio segments in *Making Connections* may surprise you. Keep in mind that they pick up a lot from contextual clues and also as they gain familiarity with the speakers. Don't worry if they think the speakers talk too quickly. As their listening skills improve, they will soon imagine that the speakers have actually slowed down!

Contents of the text

Each lesson presents a short conversation or monologue that models a real social interaction. The speakers were not given scripts, nor was the conversation limited to specific vocabulary. In other words, this is "simulated authentic language." Each lesson is accompanied by written exercises. The romanization system used in this text is *pinyin*, with tone marks included.

CD #1: 23 lessons

The order and topics of these lessons are coordinated to go with the lessons in *Integrated Chinese*, Level I, Parts 1 & 2. While *Making Connections* is an ideal accompaniment to that text, it need not only be used in that way. It can certainly stand alone as a listening comprehension component to courses that use other texts or for self-learners or heritage students who already have some background in Mandarin.

CD #2: 22 lessons

These lessons are of a different nature from those in the first CD. Whereas the first CD presents conversations between the same two speakers, the second CD offers students a chance to hear a variety of speakers talking about a wide range of subjects. For the most part, these conversations or monologues are set in the United States; six lessons (Lessons 24-28, and 31) are set in China. Three lessons (Lessons 40, 41, 45) are Chinese-language radio broadcasts that probably would take place outside of China or Taiwan. Like the first CD, these audio segments are naturally-paced and unscripted. The lessons are arranged so that they become progressively more challenging, ranging in difficulty from novice- to intermediate-high levels of proficiency. A rough distribution of the levels is as follows:

Level I (Novice-high)   Lessons 24-31 (CD #2, segments 1-8)

Level II (Intermediate)   Lessons 32-37 (CD #2, segments 9-14)

Level III (Intermediate/High-Advanced)   Lessons 38-45 (CD #2, segments 15-22)

Instructors should note that although the levels of the segments may at first seem too high for your students, the exercises given in the lessons will help them negotiate and apply listening comprehension strategies they learned in CD #1 to these more complex conversations. Keep in mind that there is no expectation for them to grasp every word or nuance. The exercises for these lessons are intentionally challenging and incorporate words and phrases that may or may not have been previously introduced. The purpose of this approach is to give students a chance to move beyond their current level of mastery to figure out what the speakers are saying, based on context and other hints given in the exercises. This is dramatically different from what most students have encountered so far in their study of Chinese, since most conventional textbooks only include words or structures that students have formally learned and that are accepted as "perfect" Chinese speech. Students may think their progress is slow-going, and the exercises at first might seem daunting, but soon they will discover how much better prepared they are to encounter situations in which authentic Chinese is spoken. For this reason, the lessons on CD #2 are particularly useful and motivating for students who are preparing to go abroad or to continue with more advanced-level Chinese courses.

Students who have completed most of the lessons on CD #1 and are familiar with the format and expectation of the lessons are well equipped to start using the more challenging material on CD #2. Some of the topics on this CD are: Going to the Market, A Traffic Accident, Apartment Hunting, A Tour of Universal Studios, Sightseeing in China, and Interviewing a Physically Disabled Student (for a complete listing, see the Table of Contents). As is readily apparent from the titles of some of these lessons, in addition to gaining competence in understanding spoken Mandarin, students will also become familiar with important aspects of Chinese culture as they work with this material.

The final eight lessons are more advanced, which offers students the benefit of being able to continue their listening comprehension development even beyond the level of their main text. After students develop the listening comprehension base that *Making Connections* encourages, these upper-level lessons offer them a challenge and a resource for continued skill development. Several of the speakers in these later lessons have slight regional accents, and their language usage is not always grammatically perfect. Nonetheless, these lessons provide students a chance to practice listening to slightly non-standard Chinese, since inevitably they will have to face this situation. Instructors are urged to be tolerant with these materials and avoid the tendency to focus on what the speakers should have said. Rather, if students follow what is emphasized in the lesson, they will profit greatly from exposure to this type of Chinese.

Please note that more Chinese is used in the exercises in some of the more advanced lessons on CD #2 (especially Parts III and IV). This is in response to requests from instructors and students who prefer to work more in the target language. This approach lends variety and flexibility to the learning process.

Organization and structure of each lesson

Each lesson is divided into five parts:

Part I. Preparation

This section should be used before students listen to the audio segment. Generally it consists of two parts. One part offers **useful vocabulary** that relates to the topic in the lesson. Whenever possible, visual cues help introduce vocabulary—students are asked to match the Chinese characters (sometime accompanied by *pinyin*) to the appropriate picture. Students are presented with additional limited vocabulary through short definitions in English (or Chinese when possible). Some idiomatic expressions with sample sentences showing usage are also given.

The second part of the pre-listening activities provides the context for the audiotext by using advance organizers[1] to activate students' background knowledge on the topic to be discussed. Brief exercises are offered to personalize and contexualize the vocabulary and concepts introduced in the dialogue and prepare students for active listening. Generally a "notepad" is provided for students to jot down notes or respond to questions **in English** (if students want to add *pinyin* or Chinese, they are free to do so—this is entirely for their own use and should not be collected or "graded" by the instructor). This section is an excellent way to stimulate classroom conversation (which may be conducted in Chinese or English, according to the instructional goals). At this point the instructor may want to clarify students' questions in usage or pronunciation or offer **minimum** additional vocabulary.

Part II. Listening for the Gist

In this section students are led to discover the general points of the conversation, such as the relationship between the speakers, their venue, and the main topic of conversation. These initial tasks are intentionally minimal and simple, since the emphasis is on global comprehension. The students read the questions first so they know what to listen for. If students have difficulty with this section, they should listen to the segment again.

Part III. Listening for Details

This section includes specific, task-based exercises that require greater comprehension. The exercises focus on what the speakers said and how they said it. Tasks include completion of tables and charts, multiple choice, true/false, matching, and cloze exercises. Depending on the level of difficulty, the exercises are either entirely in English or sometimes in a combination of English and simple Chinese.

Part IV. Working with the Language

This section provides students a chance to work with new vocabulary and grammar. Tasks include matching, sentence and dialogue completion, transformation exercises, cloze exercises, translation, and multiple choice. No attempt is made to cover every grammatical point or idiomatic usage that occurs in the audio segment; rather, the goal is to highlight a few important linguistic features. Often these will be items that students have learned previously but from which they may profit by seeing them presented in a different, less formal format.

Part V. Follow-up Activities 大家來說／大家來寫

This section gives students a chance to practice expressing themselves in spoken and written Chinese. Each lesson offers guided activities contextually related to the conversation. Tasks include role playing, dialogue completion, writing activities (with writing in Chinese), etc. The exercises are designed either for classroom settings or for independent work, and they are flexible enough so instructors and students can adapt them to their needs.

✳ ✳ ✳

How can *Making Connections* be integrated into your curriculum?

---

[1]Hadley defines "advance organizers" as "introductory materials at a high level of generality presented in advance of the new material to be learned." As she notes, "such organizers will facilitate the learning process by providing a kind of general anchoring idea to which the new knowledge can be attached" (Alice Omaggio Hadley, *Teaching Language in Context* [Heinle & Heinle, 1993], p. 58).

Articulation

Making Connections is especially effective in helping address the issues of articulation that are so problematic, especially at the college level. After completing a semester or a year of beginning Chinese, students are frequently worried about material they may have forgotten since the previous semester or during summer break. They may have transferred from schools that use different textbooks or emphasize different teaching/learning approaches, or they may be returning from different study-abroad programs. Instructors frequently are in the position of having to teach students with a variety of skills and backgrounds, and they are often unsure how to begin a course that will accommodate the needs of such a diverse group of students. *Making Connections* is an excellent resource for alleviating some of these concerns. When used at the beginning of the subsequent course, this workbook can refresh students' memories while at the same time presenting new and exciting material in a dynamic way. It offers common ground to all students, which will lower affective fears and create an atmosphere of high motivation.

Suggestions for use in curriculum

Model 1 — To be used with *Integrated Chinese* or other beginning/intermediate-level text

For students who have completed one semester, college level Chinese: CD#1: One lesson per week (e.g., in conjunction with *Integrated Chinese*, Level 1, Part 2). For students who have completed one academic year, college level Chinese: CD#1: 1-3 lessons per week at beginning of the academic session (e.g., in conjunction with *Integrated Chinese*, Level 2).

In class: Last 10 minutes of class period

The instructor works with students to complete pre-listening activities. This "brainstorming" session can be held in Chinese or English, depending on the students' levels. The students are encouraged to work in groups or pairs. Students are introduced to the vocabulary items in Part I of each lesson. After students have completed Part I, they read the "Listening for the Gist" exercises. Then the instructor plays the CD segment once, without stopping, and allows a few minutes for students to complete the exercises (or answer the questions). In some cases it may be necessary to play the segment a second time.

Homework assignment

Students complete Parts III and IV (they need to have access to the CD) and submit these to the instructor for correction.

In class: Follow-up (half class period)

This session could occur later in the week, ideally after student papers have been returned. The oral activities in Part V are particularly well suited to classroom settings. Additional practice with vocabulary/grammar may be included as the instructor wishes. The writing and reading activities in Part V are best assigned as homework.

Model 2 — For students who have completed two academic years of college-level Chinese

Use lessons 1-23 on CD #1 intensively at the beginning of the academic year. Students should be able to work largely on their own. The written exercises can be turned in on a weekly basis or collected in a portfolio.

The lessons on CD #2 can be assigned similarly (either one lesson per week or one lesson per two weeks) for the remainder of the year. Ideally the instructor should follow the same general model that is outlined above (i.e., working with pre-listening activities before they work with the conversations themselves). In this way teachers and students will be reminded of how integral the listening component is to their entire Chinese language curriculum. Instructors will need to decide how many of the lessons on CD #2 are appropriate for their students. Most students should be ready to proceed to Level II (lessons 32-37). Some instructors may want to save the Level III segments (lessons 38-45) for work in third- or fourth-year courses or for independent work by students who want greater challenge.

To the Student

Welcome to *Making Connections: Enhance Your Listening Comprehension in Chinese*. This book offers a dynamic and exciting way to improve your skills in understanding spoken Chinese. Whether you are a beginning student of Chinese or someone who has been learning Chinese for a long time, *Making Connections* offers a chance to work directly with "real" Chinese that is spoken at a normal pace and uses language that is natural and spontaneous.

The conversations in this text are presented in authentic, naturally-paced language, and the lessons emphasize vocabulary and structures that occur in real communication. As your competence in understanding spoken Mandarin increases, you will also become familiar with the *ways* people speak to each other and some of the subtleties of language and culture that make Chinese distinctive. The biggest difference you will find in working with *Making Connections*, as opposed to your main textbook, is that there are no long lists of vocabulary to memorize and there is no written version of each conversation. Although this may be somewhat disconcerting at first, you will soon see the advantages to this approach. One of the skills you need to develop is that of anticipating what a speaker might say and then verifying whether you are right. This kind of "interactive listening" will keep you engaged in the conversation, even though you won't understand every single word.

Keep in mind that you are not expected to understand or remember every word you hear. What seems initially confusing will become clear as you complete the exercises. It will be challenging at first and maybe even frustrating, but if you stick with it, you'll find a strong positive shift in your way of approaching listening comprehension. Before long you'll be more confident in your own conversations with speakers of Chinese.

Making Connections consists of two kinds of lessons. CD #1 has conversations between two Chinese graduate students who are studying in the United States. Once you have completed most of the lessons on CD #1 and are familiar with the format and expectation of the lessons, you will be ready to start using the more challenging material on CD #2, which features 22 dialogues, interviews, or monologues on a range of topics and uses different speakers, so that you can get used to hearing a variety of male and female voices. The written exercises will guide you through each audio segment. Simply complete the tasks in each section of the lesson and you'll have no trouble learning with this text. The lessons become increasingly challenging, so don't get discouraged. Level II is appropriate for students who have had at least two years of college-level Chinese courses. Level III offers practice to advanced students who want to work with more demanding materials.

A rough distribution of the levels is as follows:

Level I   Lessons 24-31 (CD #2, segments 1-8)

Level II Lessons 32-37 (CD #2, segments 9-14)

Level III Lessons 38-45 (CD #2, segments 15-22)

Several of the speakers in these lessons have slight regional accents, and their language usage is not always grammatically perfect. Nonetheless, these lessons offer you a chance to practice listening to slightly non-standard Chinese that usually you only encounter after you've gotten off the plane in China or Taiwan or that you hear when Chinese speakers speak to one another. The exercises for these lessons are intentionally challenging and incorporate words and phrases that you may or may not have previously learned formally. Try making educated guesses based on the context given in the conversation and other clues given in the exercises. Remember you need not master every word that is spoken. This approach might be dramatically different from what you are used to, so it may be disconcerting at first. But if you stick with it, you'll find your listening comprehension will improve substantially. Here's a listening strategy that will help you work with these materials.

Each lesson is divided into five parts:

Part I. Preparation

This section will prepare you with some **useful vocabulary** relevant to the topic on the audio segment. Some of the vocabulary you may have learned before, but this is a good chance to make sure that you really know what these terms mean. You will also see some idiomatic expressions with sample sentences showing usage. Make sure you understand these example sentences; occasionally you will be asked to write down translations into English.

The second part of the activities that you should do **before you listen to the audio segment** is answer the question that relates your personal experience with the topic of the lesson. Generally a "notepad" is provided for you to jot down your responses **in English.** Of course, feel free to add notes in Chinese (*pinyin* or characters) if you want, but don't spend a lot of time on this section. This section is for your own reference and will not be "graded" by your instructor.

Part II. Listening for the Gist

Now you are ready to listen to the audio segment for the first time. Before listening, look over the questions that appear in this section. You should be able to answer most of these questions after listening to the conversation only once or twice.

Listen generally; try to capture the main idea of the conversation. Don't get bogged down trying to grasp too many specific details. Remember, this is just the first time you are hearing the conversation—you'll have plenty of chances to work with specifics later.

Part III. Listening for Details

Listen to the conversation again.

You're on your own now. You can listen to the conversation as many times as you need to. Try to listen to it all the way through, rather than pausing after each utterance. **Hint:** Read the exercises first so you know what information you are listening for. If there are unfamiliar words in the exercises you might want to consult a dictionary before you listen to the conversation again.

Now you're ready to complete the exercises in this section.

Part IV. Working with the Language

This section gives you a chance to work with some vocabulary and grammatical patterns that might be unfamiliar. The exercises are based on vocabulary and grammatical patterns used in the conversation. This section can be done without listening to the tape again.

Part V. Follow-up Activities 大家來說／大家來寫

This section allows you to express yourself orally and in writing based on the material you have learned by listening to and working with this conversation. It is best to work on these activities after you have completed all the other sections. Sometimes you might want to listen to the conversation again to give you some ideas, but this is your chance to be creative and take a few risks!

ABBREVIATIONS

Adj	adjective
Adv	adverb
Coll	colloquial
Conj	conjunction
MW	measure word
N	noun
Nu	number
Ph	phrase
PRC	People's Republic of China usage
Prep	preposition
Suf	suffix
TW	Taiwan usage
V	verb
V O	verb-object

Lesson 1 第一课
Greetings 问好

 **Preparation**

Useful vocabulary

系	xì	N	department (e.g., 英文系，中文系，历史系)
前	qián	N	(前头 qiántou／前面 qiánmian)
后	hòu	N	(后头／后面)
上	shàng	N	(上面)
下	xià	N	(下面)
旁边	pángbiān	N	side
东	dōng	N	(东边)
南	nán	N	(南边)
西	xī	N	(西边)
北	běi	N	(北边)
对面	duìmiàn	N	opposite, right in front of
正好	zhènghǎo	Adv	just right; by a happy coincidence, it just turns out that, by chance, as it turns out

Example：

小张正好也要去中文系。

咱们	zánmen	N	we (including speaker; this usage occurs in northern dialects)

See if you can locate these places on the map above and say what parts of China they are in:

吉林 Jílín   北京 Běijīng   上海 Shǎnghǎi

长春 Chángchūn   香港 Xiāng Gǎng   台北 Táiběi

                   (Hong Kong)   (Taipei)

Example:

吉 Jílín 在中国的东北。

Listening for the Gist

Listen to the dialogue. Check which places are mentioned.

- ❑ Beijing.
- ❑ Changchun.
- ❑ Shanghai.
- ❑ Hong Kong.
- ❑ Taipei.

The people in this dialogue are …

- ❑ a Chinese tourist and a teacher of Chinese.
- ❑ two Chinese students from the PRC (People's Republic of China).
- ❑ two Chinese teachers from the PRC.
- ❑ a Chinese student from Taiwan and a Chinese student from the PRC.

The person who is asking for directions is …

- ❑ female.
- ❑ male.

This conversation takes place …

- ❑ on a college campus.
- ❑ at the airport.
- ❑ at a bookstore.
- ❑ at a bus station.

Listening for Details

The woman's name is … (circle one)

Li Yingwen.   Li Wenyang.
Li Wenyin.   Li Wenying.

Based on the information she gives, see if you can write the rest of her name in characters below.

李

The man's name is … (circle one)

Zhang Linshen.   Zhang Linsheng.
Zhang Lingshen.   Zhang Lingsheng.

Based on the information he gives, see if you can write the rest of his name in characters below.

张

The woman is asking directions to …

- ❑ the Department of English.
- ❑ the Department of Chinese.
- ❑ a Chinese restaurant.
- ❑ the library.

4

The person who gives directions has lived in the United States for …

❏ three years.   ❏ five years.

❏ four years.   ❏ six years.

Working with the Language

Zhang Linsheng and Li Wenying were talking about how American campuses were laid out differently from Chinese campuses. He happened to have a map of the Beijing University and was showing it to Li Wenying. A small part of this map has been reproduced on the 非). A gloss to some of the place names is given below.

未名	wèi míng	unnamed
湖	hú	lake
楼	lóu	building
哲学	zhéxué	philosophy
体育馆	tǐyùguǎn	gymnasium
教室	jiàoshì	classroom
生物（学）	shēngwù(xué)	biology
地（理）学	dìlǐxué	geography
文史	wénshǐ	literature and history
化学	huàxué	chemistry

图舒馆在未名湖的西边。   是　非

哲学楼在第二体育馆旁边。   是　非

第一教室楼的后面是生物北馆。   是　非

地学楼在文史楼跟化学楼的中间。   是　非

第一体育馆正好在第二体育馆对面。   是　非

文史楼前头就是地学楼。   是　非

未名湖离第一体育馆不远。   是　非

图书馆旁边没有教室。   是　非

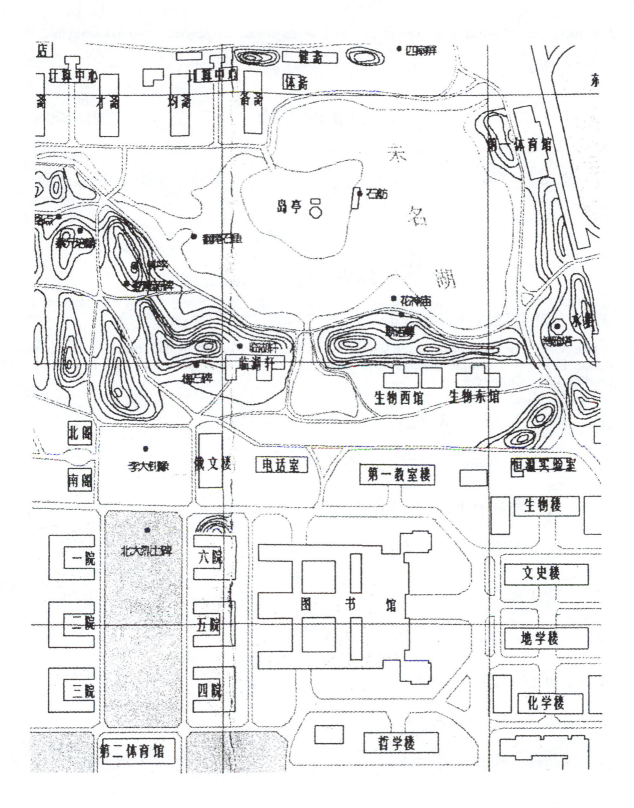

Complete the following short paragraph using words or expressions from the following list:

高兴　　刚　　认识　　好像　　中文系　　正好　　英文系

小李跟小张以前不＿＿＿＿＿＿。他们两个人都是 ＿＿＿＿＿＿ 的研究生 (yánjiū-shēng, yánjiùshēng: graduate students)。小李＿＿＿＿＿ ＿＿＿＿＿到美国，＿＿＿＿＿＿她有一点寂寞 (jímò, jìmò: lonely)。今天她 ＿＿＿＿＿＿ 看到了小张，所以她现在很＿＿＿＿＿＿。

➷ Follow-up Activities

大家来说 Role-playing (oral)

With a partner practice introducing yourself in Chinese. Be sure to explain how to write your name. Below is a sample dialogue you might want to use as a guideline. First take turns reading this dialogue aloud.

王：　我姓王，叫王友生。

高：　王先生，你好！你的名字怎么写？

王：　友就是朋友的友。生是医生的生。

高：　这个名字真好听！我姓高，我叫高英美。

王：　"Ying" 是什么"Ying"？

高：　"Ying" 是英国的英，"Mei" 是美国的美。

王：　高小姐，认识你很高兴！

高：　认识你也很高兴。

王：　你是什么地方来的？

高：　我是台北来的。你呢？

王：　我是上海来的。

大家来写 **Role-playing (written)**

Referring to the map, identify the name of the province (give the Chinese characters and pīnyīn) in which these cities can be found.

长沙 Chángshā

_____

天津 Tiānjīn

_____

昆明 Kūnmíng

_____

上海 Shànghǎi

_____

成都 Chéngdū

_____

青海 Qīnghǎi

_____

西安 Xī'ān

_____

长春 Chángchūn

_____

武汉 Wǔhàn

_____

哈尔滨 Hāěrbīn

_____

Lesson 2 第二课
Family 家庭

 **Preparation**

Useful vocabulary

非常	fēicháng	Adv	extraordinarily, very
全	quán	Adv	all, completely
主要	zhǔyào	Adj	for the most part, main, chief
理解	lǐjiě	V	to understand (cf. 懂)

See if you can guess the meaning of these words from the way they are used in the following sentences:

退休 tuìxiū   刚 gāng

我爸爸今年六十五岁了，他大概 (dàgài: probably) 会<u>退休</u>。

张林生<u>刚</u>来美国的时候非常想家，慢慢儿就好起来了。

Think of times when you feel homesick (xiǎng jiā 想家). What do you do to cheer yourself up? Do you think these feelings of homesickness would be different for a student from China? Why or why not? Take a few minutes to jot down some of these thoughts or share them with a partner in class.

_____

_____

_____

_____

_____

_____

_____

 **Listening for the Gist**

Why did Zhang Linsheng initiate this conversation?

☐ He had a question about coursework he wanted to ask Ms. Li.

☐ He could tell Ms. Li was unhappy.

☐ He wanted to tell Ms. Li about his family.

☐ He wanted to ask Ms. Li to have dinner.

Why is Li Wenying feeling homesick?

☐ She just got a phone call from her parents.

☐ She was looking at a picture of her daughter.

☐ She just received a letter from home.

☐ All her classmates have activities planned for the weekend.

Circle the members of Li Wenying and Zhang Linsheng's families that are mentioned in this conversation.*

Li	Zhang
grandparents	grandparents
father	father
mother	mother
younger brother	younger brother
older brother	older brother
younger sister	younger sister
older sister	older sister
husband	wife
daughter	daughter
son	son

Note: When Zhang Linsheng talks about his family, he doesn't need to use the possessive marker 的, since it is generally omitted when referring to close family members. Similarly, it is not necessary to include a measure word when referring to someone's occupation, i.e., Zhang Linsheng could have said, "我妹妹是工人。"

Listening for Details

Check all the members of Li Wenying's family that she mentions; then draw a line connecting each of them to their occupation in Column B.

Column A	Column B
grandparents	teacher
father	lawyer
mother	is retired
younger brother	doctor
older brother	worker
younger sister	college student
older sister	high school student
husband	

Where are Li Wenying's family members now living? (circle all that apply)

United States	Beijing	Harbin
Shanghai	Changchun	Nanjing

How old is Li Wenying's daughter?

☐ 一岁　　☐ 四岁　　☐ 两岁　　☐ 她没说　　☐ 三岁

Now listen to what Zhang Linsheng says about his family and then draw a line connecting each family member he mentions to their occupation in Column B.

Column A	Column B
grandparents	teacher
father	lawyer
mother	is retired
younger brother	doctor
older brother	worker
younger sister	college student
older sister	high school student
wife	

Why does Li Wenying thank Zhang Linsheng at the end of the conversation?

- ☐ Because talking to him cheered her up.
- ☐ Because he gave her some good ideas about how to cheer herself up.
- ☐ Because he invited her to meet his family.
- ☐ Because he showed her pictures of his family.

Working with the Language

Below are two frequently used idiomatic expressions that occurred in this dialogue: See if you can translate the following examples into English.

怪不得　　　guàibudé　　　"no wonder"

Examples:

甲：你的中文怎么说得那么好？

乙：我从小就在家里说中文。

甲：怪不得。

就是说   "that is to say . . ." (used for clarification or explanation)

甲：你的意思就是说，中文是你的母语 ("mother tongue": native language)

　　　对不对？

乙：对，可以这样说。

Complete these two dialogues using either 怪不得 or 就是说. Then translate them into English.

李：我今天非常想家。

张：为什么？

李：因为我家里的人刚给我打电话了。

张：_____你有一点不高兴。

_____

_____

_____

张：你弟弟做什么工作？

李：他又是学生，又是老师。

张：这是什么意思？

李：这_____他大学还没毕业(bìyè: to graduate)，所以还不能当

　　(dāng: to act as) 真正的老师 (zhēnzhèng: real, true)。

张：啊，我懂了。

_____

_____

_____

Follow-up Activities

 大家来说 **Role-playing (oral)**

With a partner, find out about each other's family. For example, you could ask how many brothers and sisters s/he has,* how old they are, what do they do, where do they live, how often does s/he call or write them. Be sure to use the expressions 怪不得 and 就是说.

*Hint: the general term for brothers and sisters is 兄弟姐妹 xiōngdì jiěmèi.

大家来写 **Role-playing (written)**

Later that night Li Wenying decided to write a letter to her family. Can you help her complete it?

收到(shōudào: received) 你们的信以后，我心里_____。

我来美国已经_____月了，可是_____。

你们最近好吗？弟弟_____？

爸爸的身体 (shēntǐ: lit. "body, "health) _____

_____？妈妈的_____？

希望你们常常给我写＿＿＿＿＿＿＿＿。祝

＿＿＿＿＿＿＿＿

文英　　上

＿＿＿年＿＿＿月＿＿＿日

Lesson 3 第三课
Dates and Time 时间

 **Preparation**

Useful vocabulary

挺好 tǐng hǎo   Adv   很好

感谢 gǎnxiè   Adj   非常谢谢一个人 (often used in formal speech or written contexts)

Review these expressions — write down a situation (in English) when each could be used.

不(用)谢

_____

不(用)客气

_____

哪里哪里

_____

沒有什么了

_____

沒事(儿)

_____

那也可以

_____

What do you like to do to celebrate your birthday? List three things.

_____

_____

_____

Do you think Chinese attitudes toward celebrating birthdays are different from those of Americans? In what ways? Why do Chinese (especially older people) often eat noodles on their birthdays?

_____

_____

_____

_____

_____

_____

_____

_____

_____

_____

_____

_____

 **Listening for the Gist**

Listen to the conversation and check which of these expressions you hear.

	✓
不用谢	
不用客气	

	✓
哪里哪里	
沒有什么了	
沒事(儿)*	
那也可以	
感谢	
你太客气了	

*People from Northern China (especially Beijing) often add 儿 ér endings. If you listen closely, you'll notice that Zhang Linsheng, who is from Beijing, sometimes pronounces words in this way.

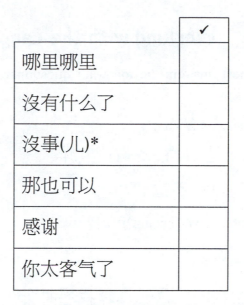 Listening for Detail

How did Li Wenying find out when Zhang Linsheng's birthday is?
- ❑ From his wife.
- ❑ From his daughter.
- ❑ From a mutual friend.
- ❑ She saw the date on his passport.

Zhang Linsheng's birthday is on (circle one):

Mon. Tues. Wed. Thurs. Fri. Sat. Sun.

What is the date of his birthday?
- ❑ June 29.
- ❑ June 26.
- ❑ September 26.
- ❑ September 29.

What kind of food do they decide to eat?
- ❑ Chinese.
- ❑ American.
- ❑ Thai.
- ❑ Korean.
- ❑ Japanese.

What time do they decide to meet?
- ❑ 6:00 p.m.
- ❑ 6:30 p.m.
- ❑ 7:00 p.m.
- ❑ 7:30 p.m.

Where is the restaurant located?
- ❑ Next to her house.
- ❑ Next to his house.
- ❑ Across the street from her house.
- ❑ Across the street from his house.

Working with the Language

Which of the responses best answers the following questions? Check all that are appropriate.

你最近怎么样? (Nǐ zuìjìn zěnme yàng?)

☐ 很忙　　☐ 好玩　　☐ 挺好

☐ 很快　　☐ 不错

你找我有事吗？ (Nǐ zhǎo wǒ yǒu shì ma?)

☐ 我想吃美国饭。　　☐ 我想请你们全家去吃饭。

☐ 我想请你帮我的忙。　　☐ 我想谢谢你。

Below are some phrases that generally would elicit a polite response. Which of the expressions would be best to say in each situation? Sometimes more than one response will work. Check all that apply.

	不用谢	不用客气	哪里哪里
因为和你聊天，我现在舒服多了。			
你真是一个好人。			
我想好好感谢你一下。			
我要请你去吃饭。			
你做的菜非常好吃。			
谢谢你帮助我学中文。			
你的中国话说得挺好。			

Note: Remember that 帮助 can be a verb or a noun, whereas 帮忙 is always a verb + object. So when Li Wenying says, "你给了我不少帮忙," she made a grammatical mistake. What should she have said?

 **Follow-up Activities**

大家来说 **Role-playing (oral)**

A. After hanging up the phone, Zhang Linsheng told his wife about his conversation with Li Wenying. She suggested that they eat later, since she has to work late that evening. With a partner "recreate" this conversation.

B. Later that evening Zhang Linsheng called Li Wenying back again to revise their plans. With a partner "recreate" this conversation.

大家来写 **Role-playing (written)**

Zhang Linsheng wrote a note to his wife telling her about the plans he had made with Li Wenying. What might this note say?

Lesson 4 第四课
Hobbies 爱好

 **Preparation**

Useful vocabulary

玩（玩儿）wán (wár)　　　V　　　to have fun, to enjoy, to play

Examples:

See if you can translate these sentences into English. Pay special attention to each usage of 玩 (玩儿).

1. 小张觉得周末应该去玩一玩。

2. 踢足球很好玩。

3. 小张也喜欢玩电脑。(diànnǎo: computer)

4. 他告诉他的美国朋友，北京可以玩的地方很多。

原来　　　　yuánlái　　　Adv　　1. previously, in the past, originally

　　　　　　　　　　　　　　　　　2. it turns out that, as it turns out

Examples:

1. 原来你在中国的时候喜欢玩什么呢？

What did you used to like to do for fun when you were in China?

2. 李文英原来不会游泳，怪不得她不想到海边去。

It turns out that Li Wenying doesn't know how to swim. No wonder she doesn't want to go to the beach.

轻松　　　　qīngsōng　　　Adj　　relaxed

活动　　　　huódòng　　　N　　activities

Talk to your class/partner about what you each like to do in your free time. Do you think these activities would be different if you were studying abroad? In what ways?

_____

_____

_____

_____

_____

_____

_____

_____

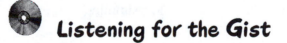 ## Listening for the Gist

Which of these topics is mentioned in this conversation? (check all that apply)
- ❑ What Xiao Li is studying.
- ❑ Kinds of movies Xiao Li likes to see.
- ❑ Kinds of sports Xiao Zhang likes to play.
- ❑ The idea of "weekend" in the U.S. and China.
- ❑ Chinese movies versus American movies.
- ❑ Activities that Xiao Li used to do in China.
- ❑ Activities that Xiao Zhang used to do in China.
- ❑ Activities that Xiao Li does in the U.S.
- ❑ Activities that Xiao Zhang does in the U.S.

In this conversation, who suggests that they do something together? (circle one)

李文英   张林生

What does s/he suggest they do?

_____

_____

🔍 Listening for Details

Where do you think this conversation takes place?

- ❑ At the library.
- ❑ At the recreation center.
- ❑ Outside a movie theater.
- ❑ At a bus stop.

What day of the week is it? (circle one)

Monday   Tuesday   Wednesday   Thursday

Friday   Saturday   Sunday

What time of day is it? (circle one)

morning   noontime   afternoon   evening

Check all the activities that Li Wenying says she used to do for fun when she was in China.

- ❑ Go to movies.
- ❑ Watch television.
- ❑ Sing.
- ❑ Read.
- ❑ Go out to eat.
- ❑ Visit friends.
- ❑ Listen to music.
- ❑ Go swimming.
- ❑ Go dancing.
- ❑ Sleep.

Check all the activities that Zhang Linsheng says he does for fun.

- ❑ Go to movies.
- ❑ Watch television.
- ❑ Go dancing.
- ❑ Play football.
- ❑ Go out to eat.
- ❑ Visit friends.
- ❑ Listen to music.
- ❑ Go swimming.
- ❑ Sleep.
- ❑ Play ping pong.

Based on the dialogue, complete the chart.

Day	
Time movie starts	
Time they will meet	
Place where they will meet	
Who else will go to the movies with them	

How does Zhang Linsheng say *Star Wars* in Chinese?

- ❑ 星星大战　　xīngxing dàzhàn
- ❑ 星球战争　　xīngqiú zhànzhēng
- ❑ 星球大战　　xīngqiú dàzhàn
- ❑ 星星战争　　xīngxing zhànzhēng

Working with the Language

Choose the verb that goes with each of these objects; in some cases there may be two verbs that are correct. Also each verb may be used more than once.

唱　打　念　看　跳　吃　听　睡　喝

Example: _____ 饭 = ___吃___ 饭

_____ 电影　　　　_____ 舞

_____ 音乐　　　　_____ 球

_____ 书　　　　　_____ 歌

_____ 水果　　　　_____ 电视

_____ 觉　　　　　_____ 汽水

Practice using 原来 yuánlái.

Usage #1. Rewrite the following sentences using 原来 … 后来 …

Example:

张林生找不到李文英。李文英在图书馆看书。

↳ 张林生原来找不到李文英，后来才在图书馆看到她。

1. 李文英来美国以前不喜欢吃美国饭。现在她觉得美国饭很好吃。

_____

_____

2. 张林生去年常常带他女儿去玩。今年他特别 (tèbié: especially) 忙，又得教书又得上课 (jiāoshū: to teach)。

_____

_____

3. 小李的先生上高中的时候住在北京。他上大学以后住在长春。

_____

_____

Usage #2. Based on the situations described above, use 原来 meaning "it turns out that" to complete these sentences.

Example:

李文英下午不在家，_____。

↳ … 原来在图书馆看书。

1. 小李在中国吃的美国饭。原来_____

_____。

2. 张林生今年很少带他女儿去玩，原来是因为 _____

_____。

3. 我以为小李的先生住在北京，原来_____

_____。

⇨ Follow-up Activities

大家来说 Role-playing (oral)

Below are newspaper clippings about several movies that are showing. Decide with a partner what movie you will see, then decide on which showing, where you will meet, and what time you will meet.

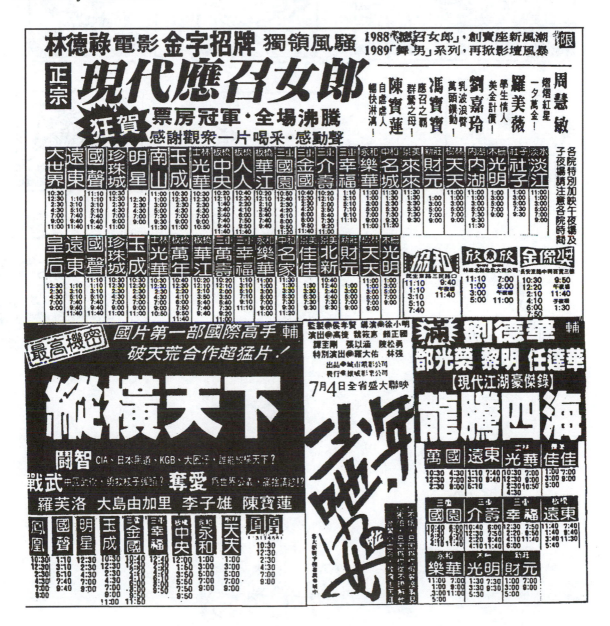

大家来写 **Role-playing (written)**

Write a brief essay describing what you do on the weekends and during the week. Include at least five of the activities depicted in the pictures below.

Lesson 5 第五课
Visiting Friends 看朋友

 Preparation

Identify the following beverages using the appropriate Chinese characters:

_____   _____   _____   _____

_____   _____   _____   _____

茶　　chá　　可乐　kělè　　汽水　qìshuǐ　　牛奶　niúnǎi

果汁　guǒzhī　　啤酒　píjiǔ　　咖啡　kāfēi

水　　shuǐ (also called 开水* kāishuǐ or 白开水 báikāishuǐ)

***Note:** Kāi means "boiled" here. Keep in mind that people don't drink tap water in China.

Here is some additional useful vocabulary that you will hear in the dialogue:

待一会儿　　dài yì huǐ(r)　　Coll　　等一会儿 děng yì huì(r), in a little bit, in a short while (cf. děng yí xià 等一下)

聊天　　　liáotiān　　V　　说话

习惯　　　xíguàn　　V　　to grow accustomed to

　　　　　　　　　N　　a habit

Examples: See if you can translate these sentences into English.

小李不习惯天天喝咖啡。

_____

她也沒有喝啤酒的习惯。

_____

流行　　　liúxíng　　Adj　　to be popular, to be trendy (refers to inanimate

　　　　　　　　　V　　objects or abstract ideas, never to people)

Examples: See if you can translate these sentences into English.

最近很流行穿黑色的衣服。

_____

中国人现在流行看美国电影。

_____

 **Listening for the Gist**

Where do you think Xiao Li And Xiao Zhang have just returned from?

- ❑ A movie theater.
- ❑ Another classmate's dorm room.
- ❑ School.
- ❑ A video store.

Where does most of this conversation take place?

- ❑ At Xiao Li's apartment.
- ❑ In the car.
- ❑ At Xiao Zhang's apartment.
- ❑ In another classmate's dorm room.

🔍 Listening for Details

How many times has Xiao Zhang's daughter seen this movie?

- ❑ Once.
- ❑ Twice.
- ❑ Three times.
- ❑ Four times.

What comments does Xiao Li make about Xiao Zhang's apartment? (check all that apply)

- ❑ It is large.
- ❑ It is new.
- ❑ It is clean.
- ❑ He has a lot of books.
- ❑ He has a good selection of music.

Which of the following does Xiao Zhang offer her to drink? (check all that apply)

- ❑ Tea.
- ❑ Juice.
- ❑ Coffee.
- ❑ Soda.
- ❑ Beer.
- ❑ Water.

Write what she decides to drink in Chinese characters.

_____

Where is Xiao Zhang's wife?

- ❑ At work.
- ❑ At the store.
- ❑ At school.
- ❑ At the library.

What does Xiao Zhang suggest they do ...

	... before his wife returns?	... after his wife returns?
Have something to drink.		
Have a snack to eat.		
Listen to music.		
Watch TV.		
Look at books.		
Chat.		
Prepare 饺子 (jiǎozi) for dinner.		
Play with his daughter.		

Which of the following expressions did Xiao Zhang and Xiao Li use to describe the movie? (circle all that apply)

非常有意思   挺好   不太好   不错   非常幽默 (yōumò: humorous)

沒有意思   很好   很流行   很无聊 (wúliáo: boring)

Working with the Language

Do you remember the difference between 有意思， 沒有意思，不好意思， and ... 的意思? See if you can fill in the blanks below with the appropriate expression. Then translate the paragraph into fluent English.

看完了电影，小张请小李来他家吃饭。张太太还没回来，所以小李有一点_____。小张的书非常多，除了中文书以外，还有英文书和日文书。小李觉得这些书都很_____，可是她不懂日文书名_____ _____。因为小张觉得看电视_____所以他们两个人就一边聊天，一边等张太太回来。

_____

_____

_____

_____

_____

_____

_____

✳ ✳ ✳

Fill in the blanks using an expression from the list below.

不过   流行   待(一)会儿   习惯   聊天   等等

1. 小李不 _____ 美国的生活。(shēnghuó: life)

2. 她 _____ 要给她朋友打电话_____。

3. 小张的女儿要跟她爸爸去看一部很 _____ 的电影。

32

Follow-up Activities

大家来说 **Role-playing (oral)**

Divide into groups of three and imagine the conversation that will take place after Xiao Zhang's wife returns. Each speaker should have at least five lines.

大家来写 **Role-playing (written)**

Below is a movie schedule. Answer the questions based on the information in this ad.

What is the name of the film advertised??

_____

How many times will it play at the Méihuā 梅花 movie theater?

_____

If you wanted to see the film at 6:00 p.m., which theater would you go to?

_____

What is the latest time you could see this film? Which theater would you go to?

_____

Which shows are discounted (hint 特价 tèjià: special price)? How much do tickets for these shows cost?

_____

Where did this film have record-breaking sales?

- ❑ 台湾
- ❑ 日本
- ❑ 美国
- ❑ 韩国

Which movie company produced this film?

- ❑ 中央电影公司
- ❑ 天空之城
- ❑ 日本电影公司
- ❑ 龙猫电影公司

Now you are ready to design your own ad for a film. Be sure to include the same type of information that was in the ad given above. You could also add the name of the director, lead actors/actresses, or any other information you think would be of interest.

Lesson 6 第六课
Studying Languages – Part 1 学语言

 **Preparation**

What do you think is most important to do when studying a foreign language? Please rank the following activities in the spaces provided (1=most important; 8=least important).

Memorize new vocabulary. _____

Listen to audio tapes or CDs. _____

Watch videotapes or DVDs. _____

Study grammar. _____

Visit the country where the language is spoken. _____

Practice speaking. _____

Practice writing. _____

Use computer-based language learning programs. _____

 **Listening for the Gist**

What is Xiao Zhang doing when he runs into Xiao Li?

❑ Studying in the library. ❑ Listening to audio tapes.

❑ Grading papers. ❑ Running some errands.

Why are they discussing dates and times?

❑ They are arranging when to have lunch.

❑ They are arranging when to take a class together.

❑ They are arranging when to go shopping.

❑ They are arranging when to go to the movies.

Listening for Details

Xiao Li thought Xiao Zhang was listening to …

❑ Japanese language tapes.

❑ English language tapes.

❑ music.

On the calendar below, mark which days Xiao Zhang has Japanese lessons this month. Today is marked.

MEMO	日/SUN	一/MON	二/TUE		三/WED	四/THU	五/FRI	六/SAT
					1 三十	2 九月初一	3 初二	4 初三
	5 初四	6 初五 今天	7 初六		8 初七 寒露	9 初八	10 初九 或雪注	11 初十
	12 十二	13 十二	14 十三		15 十四	16 十五	17 十六	18 十七
	19 十八	20 十九	21 二十		22 廿一	23 廿二 霜降	24 廿三	25
	26 廿五	27 廿六	28 廿七		29 廿八	30 廿九	31	

10 月

What time are his lessons?

- ❏ 2:00 p.m.
- ❏ 4:00 p.m.
- ❏ 2:30 p.m.
- ❏ 10:00 a.m.
- ❏ 5:00 p.m.

Why is Xiao Zhang studying Japanese?

- ❏ To do business.
- ❏ To be able to read original works of Japanese literature.
- ❏ To be able to talk to his Japanese classmates.
- ❏ To help with his studies of Chinese literature.

小李跟小张觉得学日文的时候最难的是

- ❏ 发音
- ❏ 认识字
- ❏ 语法
- ❏ 说话

Working with the Language

Which of the following comments does Xiao Li make in this conversation? (circle all that apply)

    A. 怎么学都学不好   我一点都不忙

    B. 怎么学也学不好   我一点也不忙

What is the difference in meaning between sentence A and sentence B?

_____

_____

_____

Please answer the following questions using the pattern: 一点都（也）不.

1. 小李觉得学日文很容易吗？

_____

2. 小张今天很累 (lèi: to be tired) 吗？

_____

3. 小李喜不喜欢吃日本菜？

_____

4. 日文的语法小李都懂吗？

_____

 # Follow-up Activities

大家来说 Role-playing (oral)

Xiao Zhang called his Japanese tutor that night to tell him about Xiao Li's interest in learning Japanese. With a partner enact this conversation. Be sure to explain Xiao Li's background and schedule. (The tutor's Chinese is perfect!)

大家来写 Role-playing (written)

Later Xiao Zhang and Xiao Li decided since their levels are different it would be better for them to take lessons separately. Xiao Li sent a note to the tutor explaining this situation and setting up an appointment for her first class. Please help her write this note. Be sure to include the place and times she can meet.

Lesson 7 第七课
Studying Languages – Part 2 学语言

 **Preparation**

Identify the following actions using the appropriate Chinese characters:

听广播	tīng guǎngbō	
看电视	kàn diànshì	
看报纸	kàn bàozhǐ	
看照片	kàn zhàopiàn	
照像	zhàoxiàng (also 拍照[片] pāi zhào[piàn])	
著急	zhāojí, zháojí	to be worried or concerned

Additional useful vocabulary

什么的	等等	N	and the like, and so on, etcetera.
兴趣	xìngqù	N	interest (to be interested in: 对 ＿＿＿ 有兴趣；对＿＿＿ 感 gǎn 兴趣)
越来越	yuè lái yuè …	Conj	more and more

Examples:

1. N 越来越 ＋ v/adj

小李越来越喜欢说英文。   Xiao Li likes speaking English more and more.

小李的功课越来越难。   Xiao Li's schoolwork is getting more and more difficult (or is getting harder).

2. V 得越来越 ＋ v/adj

她翻译得越来越快。   She translates more and more quickly.

3. V O V 得越来越 ＋ v/adj

小李说英文说得越来越好。   Xiao Li is speaking English better.

专业	zhuānyè	N	major/speciality
感觉	gǎnjué	N	feeling
根本	gēnběn	Adv	basically, fundamentally
进步	jìnbù	N	progress

What do you find most challenging about studying Chinese? (check all that apply)

❑ Remembering new words.

❑ Learning grammar.

❑ Writing characters.

❑ People speak too fast.

❑ People have accents that are hard to understand.

❑ Learning complex characters.

❑ Learning simplified characters.

How do you think learning Chinese compares to learning other languages and to learning English as a second language? List three specific examples of what is different about studying Chinese. Then list three things that are the same no matter what language is being studied.

Same	**Different**

Listening for the Gist

The main topic of this conversation is:

- ❑ Li Wenying's experiences studying English.
- ❑ Li Wenying's experiences teaching Chinese.
- ❑ Zhang Linsheng's experiences studying English.
- ❑ Zhang Linsheng's experiences studying English.

Who do you think speaks English better? Why?

_____

_____

Listening for Details

How old was she when she first started studying English?

- ❑ 4 years old.   ❑ 10 years old.
- ❑ 6 years old.   ❑ 12 years old.
- ❑ 8 years old.

Which of the following types of school does she mention?

- ❑ Elementary.   ❑ College.
- ❑ Middle school.   ❑ Graduate school.
- ❑ High school.

Based on her comments, circle whether her teacher(s) at each level she mentioned was/were Chinese or American and indicate what she says about the emphasis of the classes she took.

Type of school	Type of teacher	Emphasis	
Elementary	中国人 美国人	reading speaking writing grammar	_____ _____ _____ _____
Middle school	中国人 美国人	reading speaking writing grammar	_____ _____ _____ _____
High school	中国人 美国人	reading speaking writing grammar	_____ _____ _____ _____
College	中国人 美国人	reading speaking writing grammar	_____ _____ _____ _____

After coming to the United States, what does Xiao Li say she has done to improve her English? Check all that apply.

- ❑ Listened to the radio.
- ❑ Gone to the movies.
- ❑ Watched television.
- ❑ Made friends with Americans.
- ❑ Listened to language tapes.
- ❑ Exchanged language lessons with an American classmate.

What suggestion(s) does Xiao Li make to Xiao Zhang as a way he can improve his English? (check all that apply)

- ❑ She will introduce him to her American friends.
- ❑ He should watch more American TV.
- ❑ He should play soccer with her and her American friends.
- ❑ He should play basketball with her and her American friends.
- ❑ He should try to speak only English with his classmates.

Working with the Language

Here are two ways to say "I am interested in ..."

我对_____有兴趣

我对_____感兴趣

Distinguish this from

_____(很)有意思

Listen to the conversation again and indicate how many times these expressions are used and by whom.

	# of times spoken	spoken by Li	spoken by Zhang
我对_____有兴趣			
我对_____趄兴趣			
_____很有意思			

Based on the following pictures, which expression would you use? In some cases you may be able to use both.

Example:

这个比赛 (bǐsài: competition)　　她对运动有兴趣　　　很有意思

_____　　_____　　_____

_____　　_____　　_____

越来越 v/adj

Activity

Create one sentence using 越来越 based on the following information.

Example:

小张以前买的书很便宜。现在他买的书很贵。

↳小张买的书越来越贵。

1. 小李去年不会跳舞。她现在跟几个朋友学跳舞。

_____

2. 小张每天练习踢足球。他进步了很多。

_____

3.小李住在中国的时候，觉得中国电影沒有意思。她来美国以後就很喜欢看中国电影了。

_____

Follow-up Activities

大家来说 Role-playing (oral)

Xiao Zhang's wife has decided she really wants to learn English better. If you were Xiao Zhang, what kind of advice would you give her?

大家来写 **Role-playing (written)**

The next day Xiao Li introduced Xiao Zhang to one of her American friends who speaks Chinese. Here's what they said. Imagine you are David Mathews and complete the dialogue. Make sure that you explain how long you've been studying Chinese; ask Zhang how long he studied English, what he thinks is most challenging about studying foreign languages, etc.

李　　我给你们介绍一下，这是我的同学张林生，这位是

　　　　我的美国朋友 , Eric Davis.

张　　你好!

Davis:　你好。你来美国多久了？

张　　已经五年多了。你学中文学了多久？怎么说得这么好？

Davis:　哪里哪里，我 ＿＿＿＿＿＿＿＿＿＿＿＿＿＿＿＿

＿＿＿＿＿＿＿＿＿＿＿＿＿＿＿＿＿＿＿＿＿＿＿＿＿＿

＿＿＿＿＿＿＿＿＿＿＿＿＿＿＿＿＿＿＿＿＿＿＿＿＿＿

＿＿＿＿＿＿＿＿＿＿＿＿＿＿＿＿＿＿＿＿＿＿＿＿＿＿

＿＿＿＿＿＿＿＿＿＿＿＿＿＿＿＿＿＿＿＿＿＿＿＿＿＿

＿＿＿＿＿＿＿＿＿＿＿＿＿＿＿＿＿＿＿＿＿＿＿＿＿＿

＿＿＿＿＿＿＿＿＿＿＿＿＿＿＿＿＿＿＿＿＿＿＿＿＿＿

＿＿＿＿＿＿＿＿＿＿＿＿＿＿＿＿＿＿＿＿＿＿＿＿＿＿

＿＿＿＿＿＿＿＿＿＿＿＿＿＿＿＿＿＿＿＿＿＿＿＿＿＿

＿＿＿＿＿＿＿＿＿＿＿＿＿＿＿＿＿＿＿＿＿＿＿＿＿＿

＿＿＿＿＿＿＿＿＿＿＿＿＿＿＿＿＿＿＿＿＿＿＿＿＿＿

＿＿＿＿＿＿＿＿＿＿＿＿＿＿＿＿＿＿＿＿＿＿＿＿＿＿

＿＿＿＿＿＿＿＿＿＿＿＿＿＿＿＿＿＿＿＿＿＿＿＿＿＿

＿＿＿＿＿＿＿＿＿＿＿＿＿＿＿＿＿＿＿＿＿＿＿＿＿＿

Lesson 8 第八课
School Life 学校生活

 **Preparation**

Useful vocabulary

选	xuǎn	V	to choose
教书	jiāoshū	V	to teach
华侨	huáqiáo	N	overseas Chinese; foreign citizens of Chinese origin (also 华裔 huáyì)
上学	shàng xué	V	to go to school, to attend school
保重身体	bǎozhòng shēntǐ	V O	to take care of yourself, to pay attention to your health

Describe the make-up of your Chinese class. Be sure to include the number of teachers, students, females/males. Are any of your classmates 华侨?

Listening for the Gist

What does Xiao Li say is her greatest difficulty in living in the U.S.?

- ❑ She is too lonely.
- ❑ She is too tired.
- ❑ She misses her daughter.
- ❑ She is too busy.
- ❑ She can't get used to the pace of life in the U.S.

Is Xiao Zhang sympathetic to her problem? How do you know?

_____

_____

Check all the topics that were mentioned in this conversation:

	✓
Li Wenying's graduate studies.	
Li Wenying's teaching responsibilities.	
Zhang Linsheng's teaching responsibilities.	
How often Li Wenying gets together with her students.	
What Li Wenying does to relax.	

Listening for Details

How long has Xiao Li been in the U.S. when this conversation takes place?

- ❑ 3 months.
- ❑ 6 months.
- ❑ 9 months.
- ❑ 1 year.

How many classes is Xiao Li taking this semester?

- ❑ 1.
- ❑ 2.
- ❑ 3.
- ❑ 4.

What level Chinese class is Xiao Li teaching?

- ❑ First year.
- ❑ Second year.
- ❑ Third year.
- ❑ Fourth year.

Complete the following chart that describes the makeup of the students in her class.

Female students	
Male students	
Chinese-American students	
Total number of students	

除了教书以外，小李说她还做什么？ (check all that apply)

- ❑ 在图书馆工作
- ❑ 在图书馆做研究
- ❑ 帮学生的忙
- ❑ 改 (gǎi: to correct) 作文
- ❑ 每天得上学
- ❑ 去书店买书

 Working with the Language

Circle all the words in the following narrative that have to do with time.

小张来美国已经五年了。刚来的时候他一点也不习惯。除了要一边上课一边教书以外，那个时候他还要每天在图书馆工作。后来來他慢慢习惯了。虽然现在得做的事情跟以前一样多,可是小张觉得生活越来越有意思。他常常说，如果我不这么忙，就会觉得生活太无聊。

Now translate this narrative into English.

_____

_____

_____

_____

_____

_____

_____

50

In this conversation Xiao Zhang says "一年级挺不好教的。" What does he mean?

❏ It's really not easy to teach first-year Chinese.

❏ It's really not good to teach first-year Chinese.

❏ He really doesn't like to teach first-year Chinese.

❏ Students in first-year Chinese aren't really very good.

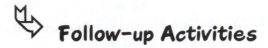 **Follow-up Activities**

大家来说 **Role-playing (oral): Interview**

Interview two students and complete the chart:

	第一个学生	第二个学生
名字		
几年级的学生		
专业		
选几门课		
选什么课		
上课的时间		
有没有工作		
工作的地方		
工作的时间		

Here is a list of Xiao Li's activities for tomorrow. Help her arrange a schedule. Please write out in Chinese characters.

She teaches Chinese (10:00-11:00 a.m.).

She helps students with pronunciation (1:00-2:00 p.m.).

She eats breakfast at 7:00, lunch at 11:30 a.m., dinner at 6:45 p.m.

She has a seminar on Chinese literature (3:30-5:50 p.m.).

She needs to prepare for her seminar on Chinese linguistics which meets the following day.

She needs to grade students' homework assignments.

She has to go to the library to check out a book.

She needs to call her husband in China (remember the time difference).

She has to buy a bus pass.

Lesson 9 第九课
Shopping 买东西

 **Preparation**

Identify the following articles of clothing using the appropriate Chinese characters:

_____ _____ _____ _____

_____ _____ _____ _____

_____ _____ _____ _____

外套	wàitào	帽子	màozi	雨伞	yǔsǎn	帶子	dàizi
衬衫	chènshān	袜子	wàzi	裙子	qúnzi	裤子	kùzi
毛衣	máoyī	鞋子	xiézi	西装	xīzhuāng	领带	lǐngdài

Additional useful vocabulary

服装	fúzhuāng	N	clothing (男装／女装)
挑	tiāo	V	to select, pick
肯定	kěndìng	Adv	definitely

 ## Listening for the Gist

How did Xiao Zhang and Xiao Li get together at the store?
- ❑ They arranged to meet there.
- ❑ They just happened to run into each other.
- ❑ They took the bus there together after class.

Which of them has already made purchases?

❑ 李文英   ❑ 张林生

What do they decide to do at the end of their conversation?
- ❑ Continue shopping.   ❑ Get something to drink.
- ❑ Get something to eat.   ❑ Go home.

Listening for Details

Which of the items given above has Xiao Li purchased:

- ❑ 外套
- ❑ 裙子
- ❑ 帽子
- ❑ 毛衣
- ❑ 袜子
- ❑ 鞋子

Which item's color does she mention?

- ❑ 外套
- ❑ 裙子
- ❑ 帽子
- ❑ 毛衣
- ❑ 袜子
- ❑ 鞋子

Which items does Xiao Zhang say he wants to buy?

- ❑ 外套
- ❑ 毛衣
- ❑ 帽子
- ❑ 鞋子
- ❑ 袜子
- ❑ 领带
- ❑ 西装

What is Xiao Li's favorite color?

- ❑ 蓝色
- ❑ 红色
- ❑ 黄色
- ❑ 紫色
- ❑ 绿色
- ❑ 灰色

What did Xiao Li buy for her daughter?

- ❑ 毛衣
- ❑ 外套
- ❑ 鞋子
- ❑ 裙子
- ❑ 袜子
- ❑ 帽子

What size shoes does Xiao Zhang wear?

- ❑ 8
- ❑ 8 ½
- ❑ 9
- ❑ 9 ½
- ❑ 10

Working with the Language

Choose the proper measure word for each of these items from the list given below. Keep in mind that some items can have more than one correct measure word.

位　条　门　件　个　把　部　本　只
双　杯　枝　封　瓶　节　套　间　张 顶

_____	外套	_____	帽子
_____	雨伞	_____	衣服
_____	衬衫	_____	袜子
_____	裙子	_____	裤子
_____	毛衣	_____	鞋子
_____	西装	_____	领带
_____	字典	_____	信
_____	铅笔	_____	茶
_____	筷子	_____	桌子
_____	电影	_____	课
_____	汽水	_____	椅子
_____	老师	_____	朋友

Note: The second time Li Wenying mentions what she bought for her daughter, she uses the generic measure word gè 个 instead of tiáo 条 or jiàn 件. Sometimes people inadvertently forget to use the more appropriate measure word and just use 个 instead. Be careful not to fall into this habit!

Degrees of certainty

Since Xiao Li is certain that the store sells the kind of shoes Xiao Zhang wishes to buy, she says 肯定有 ("they definitely have them").

Compare the range of certainty expressed by the following adverbial expressions:

肯定（一定）	definitely
大概	probably
也许 (yěxǔ), 可能	possibly
不可能	impossible
绝对/不 (juédui)	absolutely impossible, definitely doesn't

Now answer the following questions indicating an appropriate degree of certainty.

1. 小张买得到十块钱的鞋子吗？

_____

2. 小李想不想她女儿？

_____

3. 如果小张也给他女儿买一件裙子，她会很高兴吗？

_____

4. 小张可不可以穿九号的鞋子？

_____

5. 饭馆卖不卖服装？

_____

6. 外套比毛衣贵吗？

_____

7. 服装商店卖不卖裤子跟领带？

_____

8. 下雨的时候你会带雨伞吗？

_____

Follow-up Activities

大家来说 Role-playing (oral)

Xiao Li and Xiao Zhang went to the men's section of the store, where Xiao Zhang is considering purchasing a sweater, a pair of shoes, and a jacket. Xiao Li also remembered she needs to buy an umbrella. Enact a conversation in which they help each other select from the following items.

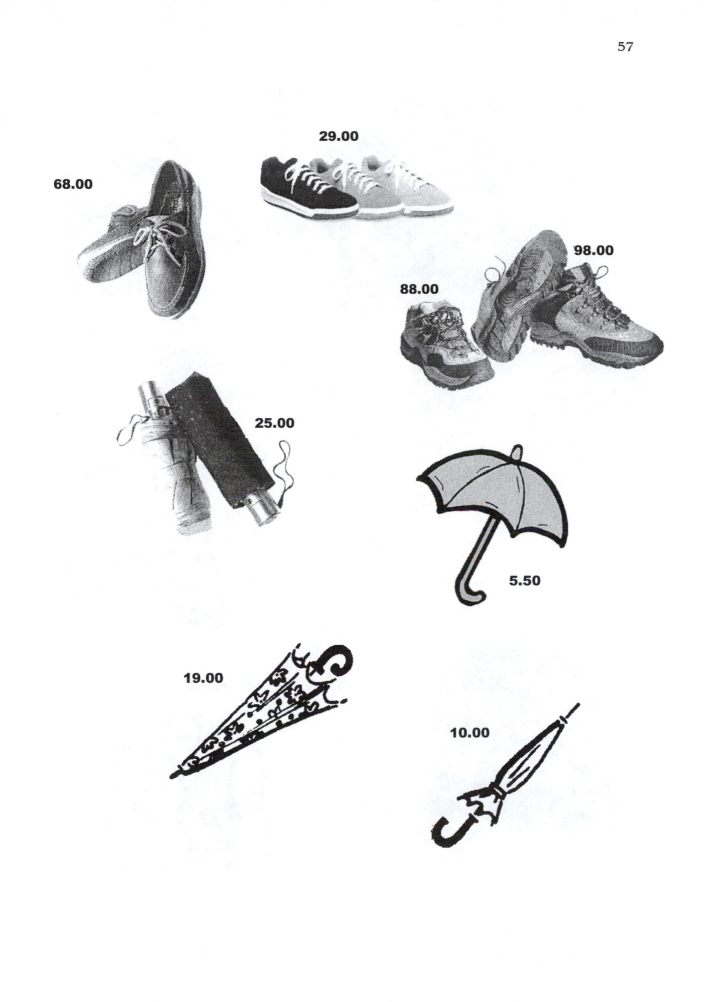

68.00

29.00

98.00

88.00

25.00

5.50

19.00

10.00

59.00

19.50

45.00

45.00

34.00

28.00

179.00

大家来写 **Role-playing (written)**

Answer the questions based on the receipts given below.

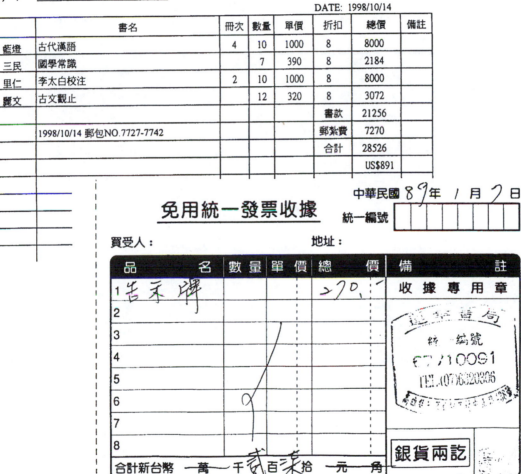

1. When were the purchases made?

_____

2. How many books were purchased?

_____

3. What was the exchange rate used in the receipt from 樂學書局 （乐学书局）?

_____

4. What is the fax number for 樂學書局?

_____

5. Who is the publisher of the book 國學常識（国学常识）?

_____

6. Which store gave a discount and how much of a discount was given?

_____

7. What do you think the characters 貳（贰）and 柒 mean in the second receipt?

_____

Lesson 10 第十课
Talking about the Weather 谈天气

 **Preparation**

Write the appropriate season 季节 (jìjié) shown in these pictures.

_____ _____

_____ _____

冬天 dōngtiān   夏天 xiàtiān

春天 chūntiān   秋天 qiūtiān

How many of these words can you use to describe the people and situations in the following pictures?

凉快	liángkuài	下雨	xiàyǔ	多云	duō yún
舒服	shūfu	下雪	xià xue	闷	mēn, mèn
潮湿	cháoshī	晴	qíng	阴	yīn
热	rè	干燥	gānzào		
冷	lěng	刮风	guā fēng		

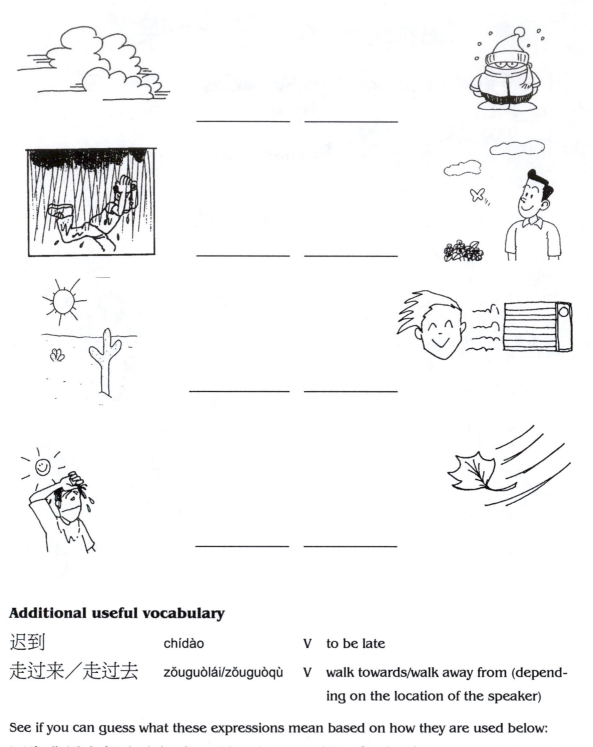

Additional useful vocabulary

| 迟到 | chídào | V | to be late |
| 走过来／走过去 | zǒuguòlái/zǒuguòqù | V | walk towards/walk away from (depending on the location of the speaker) |

See if you can guess what these expressions mean based on how they are used below:

因为我早上很晚才起床，所以上课迟到了。真对不起。

_____

_____

如果你现在有时间，就<u>走过来</u>。你家离我家很近。

_____

_____

 Listening for the Gist

Of the following topics, indicate which ones you heard mentioned in the dialogue:

	✓
Why Xiao Zhang arrived late.	
When Xiao Zhang arrived.	
Making an apology.	
The location at which they met.	
The reason for them getting together.	
The weather that day.	
The weather yesterday.	
The forecast for tomorrow.	
The weather in Beijing.	
The season with the best weather in Beijing.	
The coldest month in Beijing.	
The season the wind blows the most.	

Listening for Details

Complete the following sentences according to what you heard in the dialogue. Put a check by the correct answer.

Xiao Zhang was late because he …

	✓
lost track of time.	
missed the bus.	
couldn't start his car.	
was shoveling snow.	

How did Xiao Zhang get to school? He . . .

	✓
drove.	
walked.	
took the bus.	

What does Xiao Li say about the weather today compared with yesterday?

❑ Windy but warmer.   ❑ Very windy and snowy.

❑ Windy and colder.   ❑ Warmer and sunnier.

❑ Not as much snow but very windy.

Complete the chart describing the weather in Beijing based on what Xiao Zhang says.

	hot	cold	humid	dry	stuffy	windy	snowy	rainy	cool
winter									
spring									
summer									
fall									

In what season does he consider the weather in Beijing to be ideal?

	✓
winter	
spring	
summer	
fall	

Working with the Language

Distinguish between these two expressions:

1. 从来不 + verb

2. 从来沒 verb 过

Example:

我从来不吃肉。

我从来沒吃过日本菜。

I never eat meat. (habitual action)

I have never eaten Japanese food. (past experience)

Listen to the conversation again. Which expression does Xiao Zhang use? How many times does he use it?

_____

_____

Answer the following questions using either 从来不 or 从来沒 Be care ful － some questions can be answered with either expression but the meanings will be different.

1. 你去过內蒙古 (Nèi Měnggǔ: Inner Mongolia) 吗 ？

_____

2. 你的朋友天天喝咖啡吗？

_____

3. 你每个周末都打排球吗？

_____

4. 你的同学喜不喜欢看中国电影？

_____

Idiomatic expression:

What do you think Xiao Zhang means when he says, "北京不怎么下雪"?

- ❑ It doesn't snow that much in Beijing.
- ❑ It doesn't snow this much in Beijing.
- ❑ It's impossible for it to snow in Beijing.
- ❑ It's unlikely it will ever snow in Beijing.

Based on the pictures, compare Column B with Column A, using the pattern B 比 A + adj.
(example: 夏天比春天闷).

Column A	**Column B**

大家来说 **Role-playing (oral)**

With a partner: Compare the weather in the different seasons based on the picture. Discuss what the weather is like where you live now compared to the weather in the hometown where you grew up.

Below is a weather report. Where do you think it was published? Why?

_____

_____

台北市	多雲短暫雨	19~23°C		廣州	多雲	17~26°C
基隆北海岸地區	陰有雨	19~23°C		福州	多雲	16~22°C
台北地區	多雲短暫雨	18~23°C		重慶	陰	13~17°C
桃竹苗地區	多雲局部短暫雨	18~25°C		漢口	晴	10~20°C
台中彰化地區	多雲局部短暫雨	18~27°C		杭州	晴	10~19°C
南投地區	多雲短暫雨	18~27°C		上海	晴	12~19°C
雲林嘉義地區	多雲短暫雨	17~27°C		南京	晴	9~19°C
台南高雄地區	多雲短暫雨	20~28°C		北平	多雲	6~15°C
屏東地區	多雲短暫雨	21~29°C		開封	多雲	6~12°C
恆春半島	陰時多雲有雨	22~28°C		西安	多雲	6~12°C
宜蘭地區	陰有雨	18~22°C		洛陽	多雲	4~10°C
花蓮地區	陰時多雲有雨	20~26°C		香港	多雲	20~26°C
台東地區	陰時多雲有雨	21~28°C		東京	晴	13~21°C
澎湖地區	多雲短暫雨	21~25°C		漢城	晴	6~15°C
金門地區	多雲時晴	18~25°C		曼谷	雨	25~30°C
馬祖地區	多雲時晴	15~20°C		新加坡	雨	24~31°C
				巴黎	晴	8~12°C
				倫敦	晴	4~11°C
				紐約	陰	6~9°C
				洛杉磯	陰	17~25°C
				舊金山	陰	16~20°C
				多倫多	晴	0~7°C
				約翰尼斯堡	晴	9~26°C

今日天氣

Describe the weather in the following places (hint: 短暫 duǎnzhàn: short duration, brief, occasional):

Tainan

_____

Nanjing

_____

Hong Kong (香港 Xiānggǎng)

_____

Paris (巴黎 Bālí)

_____

大家来写 **Role-playing (written)**

That night Xiao Zhang called a Chinese friend of his who lives in California and told him about the unusual weather. Write down how you think this conversation went. Each speaker should have at least 8 lines.

_____

_____

_____

_____

_____

_____

_____

_____

_____

_____

_____

_____

_____

_____

_____

_____

_____

Lesson 11 第十一课
Transportation 交通

 Preparation

Identify the following pictures using the appropriate Chinese characters:

公路	电车	自行车／脚踏车	jiǎotàche
高速公路	汽车	出租汽／计程车	jìchéngchē
公共汽车	飞机	摩托车	mótuóche
机场(飞机场)	行李	火车	huǒche

Useful vocabulary

寒假	hánjià	N	winter break
春假	chūnjià	N	spring break
暑假	shǔjià	N	summer break
接／送	jiē/sòng	V	to meet/ to see off
麻烦	máfán	N	trouble, troublesome, bother, bothersome
危险	wēixiǎn; wéixiǎn	Adj	dangerous
办法	bànfǎ	N	method, way, means
方法	fāngfǎ	N	method, way, means
恐怕	kǒngpà	V	I'm afraid that ... I'm worried that ...;
		Adv	perhaps, possibly
提前	tíqián	Adv	in advance

How far is the airport from where you live? What is the best way to get there? How long does it take to drive there? How much does it cost to go by taxi? By bus? What are some advantages and disadvantages of each means of transportation?

	advantages	disadvantages
private car		
taxi		
bus		
other		

 **Listening for the Gist**

What did Li Wenying ask Zhang Linsheng? (check all that apply)

	✓
Driving directions to get to the airport.	
Alternatives to driving to the airport.	
If he will drive her to the airport.	
How long it takes to drive to the airport.	
If he has ever driven to the airport.	
If roads are dangerous in the snow.	

Why is she going to the airport?

❏ She is picking up her parents.

❏ She is going on a trip.

❏ She is picking up a friend.

❏ She is picking up her husband and daughter.

Listening for Details

When does Xiao Li need to go to the airport?

❏ The next day.   ❏ During spring break.

❏ During winter break.   ❏ During summer break.

Which highways does Xiao Zhang mention? (check all that apply)

❏ 36   ❏ 76   ❏ 270   ❏ 287

❏ 25   ❏ 79   ❏ 70   ❏ 225

What advantages and disadvantages do Xiao Zhang and Xiao Li mention concerning each of these transportation options?

	advantages	disadvantages
driving		
taxi		
bus		

Where is the bus station located?

❏ 15th St.

❏ 16th St.

❏ 45th St.

❏ 5th St.

Working with the Language

恐怕

Answer the following questions or respond to the situations described using 恐怕.

Example:

今天天气会怎么样？

↳ 恐怕＿＿＿＿＿会下雨。

1. 小李要去机场接她的朋友，可是她不要开车。

＿＿＿＿＿＿＿＿＿＿＿＿＿＿＿＿＿＿＿＿＿

2. 小李的朋友行李多不多？

＿＿＿＿＿＿＿＿＿＿＿＿＿＿＿＿＿＿＿＿＿

3. 下雪的时候开车危险吗？

＿＿＿＿＿＿＿＿＿＿＿＿＿＿＿＿＿＿＿＿＿

When Xiao Zhang learns that Xiao Li just learned how to drive, he says,
"要是这样的话，你最好不要开车。"
("If that is the case, it would be best for you not to drive.")

要是 ... (的话) or 如果 ... (的话) means "if."

Rewrite the following sentences using 要是 ... 的话 (or 如果 ... 的话).

Example:

下雪的时候小李不开车。

↳ 要是下雪的话，小李会坐公共汽车。

1. 坐火车比坐飞机便宜多了。

＿＿＿＿＿＿＿＿＿＿＿＿＿＿＿＿＿＿＿＿＿

2. 高速公路上，车都开得很快。

＿＿＿＿＿＿＿＿＿＿＿＿＿＿＿＿＿＿＿＿＿

3. 小李不知道公共汽车站在哪儿。

＿＿＿＿＿＿＿＿＿＿＿＿＿＿＿＿＿＿＿＿＿

Follow-up Activities

大家来说 Role-playing (oral)

With a partner: Ask about the last time you went to the airport. Why were you there? How did you get there? What is your favorite/ least favorite airport? Why?

大家来写 Role-playing (written)

This is the first time Xiao Li's friend has left China. She is planning to stay for 4 1/2 weeks. Besides visiting Xiao Li, she would like to go to Disneyland and also visit classmates who live in New York City 纽约, San Francisco 旧金山, and Chicago 芝加哥. Here is the itinerary the travel agent came up with; can you help complete it?

洛杉矶	Luòshānjī	Los Angeles
纽约	Niǔyuē	
旧金山	Jiùjīnshān	
芝加哥	Zhījiāgē	

日期	班次	目的地	登机时间	座号
12/16	UA 1146	洛杉矶	08:36am	22A

_____

_____

_____

_____

_____

_____

_____

_____

_____

Lesson 12　第十二课

Dining　吃饭

Preparation

Chinese food is usually divided into four styles of cooking—Northern, Eastern, Western, and Southern. The regions that are associated with these styles can be seen on this map.

北方菜	东方菜	西方菜	南方菜
河北	江苏	四川	广东
山西	浙江	湖南	福建
河南	安微	贵州	台湾
山东	湖北		
陕西	江西		

Wheat is a staple in Northern cooking: noodles, steamed bread and steamed buns, and ravioli-like dumplings (steamed, boiled, or fried) are frequently served. Rice is the staple in Southern cooking: steamed or fried rice, rice noodles, or sticky rice generally accompany dishes from this area. Chinese cooking emphasizes flavor, color, aroma, and presentation. Here are the main flavors in Chinese cuisine.

辣	là	hot, spicy
甜	tián	sweet
咸	xián	salty
酸	suān	sour
苦	kǔ	bitter

Additional useful vocabulary

春节	chūnjié	N	Spring Festival (Chinese New Year)
熟悉	shúxī	V	知道得很清楚
风味	fēngwèi	N	flavor
清淡	qíngdàn	Adj	light (of food)
比如	bǐrú	Adv	for example
吃素	chīsù	V O	to be a vegetarian
比较	bǐjiào, bǐjiǎo	Adv	relatively, comparatively
像	xiàng	Adv	such as; (像 … 等[等]: such as, … etc.) In formal writing 等 is used instead of 等等

Examples: See if you can translate these sentences into English in the spaces provided.

小李看过很多国家 (guójiā: country) 的电影，像美国的，日本的，法国的，还有英国的。

_____

_____

小张吃过很多种 (zhǒng: kinds, types) 中国菜，像北京菜，上海菜，四川菜，广东菜，等等。

_____

_____

要不		Conj	short for 要不然 yàobùrán: otherwise
师傅	shīfu	N	master (chef)
味道	wèidào	N	flavor, taste, smell, odor
油	yóu	N/Adj	oil, oily (can also mean cunning, slippery when describing a person)
腻	nì	Adj	greasy; bored, tired of

Example: See if you can translate this sentence into English.

我天天听那位大师傅的故事，已经听腻了。

_____

_____

What are your favorite Chinese foods? Do you know what regional style of cooking these dishes are?

_____

_____

_____

_____

_____

_____

 **Listening for the Gist**

The main topic of this conversation is …
- ❑ finding places for vegetarians to eat.
- ❑ comparing different styles of Chinese cooking.
- ❑ choosing a Chinese restaurant.
- ❑ Chinese restaurants where Li Wenying's students like to eat.

Which of the following dishes is mentioned?

			✓
糖醋鱼	tángcù yú	Sweet and Sour Fish	
家常豆腐	jiācháng dòufǔ	Family-style Tofu	
清蒸鱼	qīngzhēng yú	Steamed Whole Fish	

			✓
宫爆鸡（丁）	gōngbào jī (dīng)	Gongbao Chicken	
麻婆豆腐	mápó dòufǔ	Mapo Tofu	
红烧牛肉	hóngshāo niúròu	Braised Beef	
凉拌菜	liángbàn cài	Chinese-style Shredded Salad	
冬菇菜心	dōnggū càixīn	Black Mushrooms & Chinese Cabbage	
鱼香茄子	yúxiāng qiézi	Eggplant with Hot Garlic Sauce	

Who has a friend who is a chef? (circle one)

李文英　　　　　　　张林生

Listening for Details

Xiao Li wants to take her students out to eat because …

- ☐ the semester is almost over.
- ☐ it's almost spring break.
- ☐ it's almost Chinese New Year.
- ☐ it's almost the end of the school year.

Complete the chart based on the information given in the conversation:

	东方楼	金龙
region of cuisine		
dominant flavor		
suggested dishes		
recommended for vegetarians?		

Which restaurant does she decide to go to? (circle one)

东方楼　　　　　　　金龙

Why?

_____

_____

_____

When will the dinner be held?

❑ Thursday   ❑ Saturday

❑ Friday   ❑ Sunday

What is the chef's last name? (circle one)

王   毛   高   郑

刘   周   孔   梁

What decision is made at the end of the conversation?

❑ Xiao Zhang will order for them.

❑ Xiao Zhang will talk to the owner.

❑ Xiao Zhang will talk to the chef.

❑ Xiao Zhang will join the class for dinner.

Working with the Language

Listen to the conversation again and fill in the blanks below with the verbs that are used with these objects.

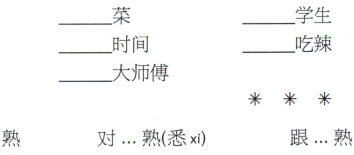

_____菜   _____学生

_____时间   _____吃辣

_____大师傅

✳ ✳ ✳

熟   对 … 熟(悉 xi)   跟 … 熟

shú/shóu*   1. to be familiar with

                2. to be ripe, to be well cooked, mature

Note: Generally speakers from Taiwan say shóu for both meanings and prefer not to use 熟悉. When 熟悉 is used as a compound, it is pronounced shúxī.

See if you can translate these sentences into English. Notice how 熟 means something different in each case.

1. 水果不熟的话就不好吃。

_____

2. 这种菜煮熟了才有味道。

_____

3. 他是我小学同学，我们两个非常熟。

_____

4. 小张对这个城市的中国饭馆很熟悉。

_____

5. 那条路小李常常走，所以她很熟。

_____

✳   ✳   ✳

每 … 都 … měi + dōu

Do you remember in this conversation when Li Wenying says "每个菜都很辣"? How would you translate her comment?

_____

_____

Rewrite the following sentences using the pattern 每 … 都 …, then translate each sentence into English.

Example:

这个饭馆的菜很辣。

↳ 这个饭馆的每个菜都很辣。

Every dish at that restaurant is spicy.

1. 我星期一到星期天吃米饭。

_____

2. 我们家对面有五个美国大学生住在一起。沒有一个人会做菜。

_____

3. 中国留学生过年的时候会想家。(liúxuéshēng: foreign student)

_____

4. 师傅希望客人吃得很高兴。

_____

5. 吃素的美国人愿意吃中国菜吗？ (yuànyì: to be willing to)

_____

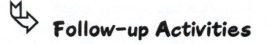

Follow-up Activities

大家来说 Role-playing (oral)

With a partner, plan a dinner for twelve people (some of whom are vegetarians) at a Chinese restaurant in your area. First compare two or three Chinese restaurants. Be sure to discuss the type of Chinese cuisine they offer, the price, location, and whether they would be able to accommodate a large party. Now design the menu, naming the specific dishes you will order.

Reading

When some of Li Wenying's students went to China recently they realized that they didn't know how to determine the kind of restaurant by the sign. One hint they discovered was that often the formal name for the region that indicated the style of cooking was given (instead of the informal name). Here are some examples:

Formal name	Informal name
鲁 Lǔ	山东 Shāndōng
湘 Xiāng	湖南 Húnán
粤 Yuè	广东 Guǎngdōng
闽 Mǐn	福建 Fújiàn
豫 Yù	河南 Hénán
蜀 Shǔ	四川 Sìchuān
沪 Hù	上海 Shànghǎi

Sometimes restaurants simply used the abbreviated form of the region. What do you think are the full names of the places indicated by these single characters:

川 Chuān _____

京 Jīng _____

港 Gǎng _____

津 Jīn _____

台 Tái _____

Here are some restaurant names and phone numbers taken from a recent Beijing public phone book.

东方沪园大酒楼	68330321
东方江湘菜美食城	6524304056
五湘斋饭庄	6512 0076
东北骨头庄饭馆	6842 1848
甘肃餐厅	6605 7398
世界屋脊青稞酒家	6401 8822 –1852 (西藏)
北京人新粤大酒楼	6801 0681
北京珠江渔村酒楼	6126 8409
醉红潮洲城	6303 6530
川好味重庆菜	6326 9682
巴蜀风大酒楼	6764 7296
鲁味餐厅	6201 5165
鲁豫餐厅	6815 7739
川鲁园餐厅	6437 3182
居德林菜馆	6404 5967 (素菜)

Answer the following questions based on these names.

1. Give the name and telephone number of the restaurant that specializes in these types of cuisine:

    a. Cantonese   _____

    b. Shanghaiese   _____

    d. Tibetan (Xīzāng)   _____

    c. Hunanese   _____

2. How many restaurants offer Sichuan-style cooking?

_____

3. Which restaurant might be most appealing to a vegetarian?

_____

4. If someone wanted to eat authentic Shandong *jiaozi*, which restaurant(s) might they try?

_____

Lesson 13 第十三课
At the Library 在图书馆

 **Preparation**

Useful vocabulary

你干嘛呢	Nǐ gànmá ne?	Coll	What are you up to?
			What are you doing?
读	dú	V	to read
半天		N	half a day；a long time
书架	shūjià	N	book shelf
查	chá	V	to look up information;
			to investigate
查字典		V	to look something up in a dictionary
电脑	diànnǎo	N	computer
情况	qíngkuàng	N	situation, circumstances; 情形
实际上	shíjìshàng	Conj	as a matter of fact (cf. shìshíshàng
			事实上, qíshí 其实 actually)
乱	luàn	Adj	disorganized, chaotic
短	duǎn	Adj	short, 不长
书名			一本书的名字
怎么办	zěnme bàn	Coll	What can be done?
没事（儿）		Coll (PRC)	"You're welcome."

How often do you go to the library? What are some of the problems you have encountered? How have you resolved them? What do you think would be the best way to improve library services on your school campus or in your community?

 **Listening for the Gist**

What is Zhang Linsheng's general mood in this conversation? Why do you think this is?

_____

_____

Check the topics that Xiao Zhang and Xiao Li mention in this conversation.

- ❑ Li Wenying's search for one particular book.
- ❑ How to use the computer to search for books.
- ❑ Why Zhang Linsheng doesn't like to go to the library.
- ❑ Hours that the library is open.
- ❑ Problems with overdue fines.
- ❑ How books are checked out in libraries in China.
- ❑ A library project Xiao Li is working on with her classmates.

Listening for Details

What is the title of the book is Xiao Li looking for?

- ❑ 中国文选史
- ❑ 中国文学史
- ❑ 中国文选
- ❑ 中国语言学史

In looking for this book, which of the following actions has Xiao Li done ?

- ❑ Checked the shelves.
- ❑ Checked the computer database.
- ❑ Asked the librarian.
- ❑ Checked inter-library loan.
- ❑ Checked the cart with books to be shelved.
- ❑ Checked to see if any of her classmates own this book.
- ❑ Checked to see if any of her classmates have checked out this book.

Which of the above options does Xiao Zhang suggest that Xiao Li do?

_____

_____

Which three things does Xiao Zhang mention that are different between this library and the one he used in China?

- ❑ In China there are no open stacks.
- ❑ The librarians are more helpful in China.
- ❑ The librarians are more helpful in the U.S.
- ❑ Libraries are open for longer hours in China.
- ❑ Libraries are open for longer hours in the U.S.
- ❑ There are more computers in libraries in the U.S.
- ❑ Libraries in China are quieter than those in the U.S.
- ❑ Libraries in the U.S. are quieter than those in China.
- ❑ Library fines in the U.S. are more expensive that those in China.

📕 Working with the Language

Fill in the blanks based on what was said in the conversation. Choose from the following words or phrases (hint: not all these words were used, and the words may be used more than once).

谁	图书馆	要是	借	同学	好
然后	拿	特别	把	虽然	帮

1. 你____书名写____给图书馆员。他会____你____书找到。

2. ____书的时间____很长，但是____过期，罚金____贵。

3. 找咱们的____看看他们____有这本书，____向他____一下。

Now translate each of the completed sentences into English.

1._____

_____

_____

2._____

_____

_____

3._____

_____

_____

How would you translate the phrase 我找了半天也没有找到?

_____

_____

Follow-up Activities

大家来说 Role-playing (oral)

That morning Lin Wenying spoke with a classmate she saw in the library and he said he'd help her track down the book she needs. That evening he called her and they talked about this issue and some of their concerns regarding the library. With a partner, enact this conversation.

大家来写 Role-playing (reading)

Based on this library card, give the following information:

Name of library _____

Gender of card holder _____

When the card expires _____

Which of the following is NOT mentioned on the back of the card?

- ❑ Hours that the library is open.
- ❑ Whether the card can be used at other libraries.
- ❑ Whether the card can be used for other purposes.
- ❑ What you should do when the card expires.
- ❑ What happens if you lend the card to someone else to use.
- ❑ What you should do if the card gets ripped or is lost.
- ❑ What someone who finds the card should do.

What year does 民國 77 年 correspond to?

- ❑ 1977
- ❑ 1987
- ❑ 1988

Do you know why?

_____

_____

_____

國 立 中 央 圖 書 館

閱 覽 證

閱覽證號	4 2032 7X71	性別	F
姓　名	白明德		
有效日期	民國 77 年 12 月 31 日		
發證日期	民國 76 年 1 月 23 日		
備　註	☑核發　□補發　□換發		

注 意 事 項

1. 憑本證、填寫閱覽記錄單後，於管制口，入繳交，出領回。
2. 應遵守本館一切閱覽規則。
3. 本證如自行塗改變換或缺少照片印章或轉借他人，均視為無效並沒收之。
4. 本證遺失或破損不堪使用時應即按照手續向本館申請補換，未辦補換手續而重領新證者，一經查出即予沒收。
5. 本證專供在本館之用，不得作為其他證明，否則一經查出，即予作廢。

Lesson 14 第十四课
Asking Directions 问路

 **Preparation**

Identify the following items using the appropriate Chinese characters.

十字路口	shízìlùkǒu		招牌	zhāopái
红绿灯	hónglǜdēng		电影院	diànyǐngyuàn
购物中心	gòuwù zhōngxīn		马路	mǎlù

Additional useful vocabulary

老板	lǎobǎn	N	owner, boss
经常	jīngcháng	Adv	常常
校园	xiàoyuán	N	campus

向 . . . 拐	xiàng … guǎi	Prep	turn in x direction at … （向左拐；向右拐）
	(or zhuǎn 转)	V	turn left, turn right at …; this usage occurs in northern dialects)
之后	zhī hòu	Suf	= 以后 （cf. 之前， 之间， 等等）
不多久	bùduōjiǔ		before very long
欢迎(你)光临	huānyíng (nǐ) guānglín	Ph	(generally occurs as 欢迎光临)

↳ "We welcome your patronage" (frequently said to customers when entering or leaving a store).

Listening for the Gist

Who recommended that Li Wenying call this place?

_____

_____

Why did Li Wenying make this call?

_____

_____

Listening for Details

Whom did Xiao Li speak with?
- ❑ 陈老板 Chén
- ❑ 郑老板 Zhèng
- ❑ 赵老板 Zhào
- ❑ 沈老板 Shěn
- ❑ 程老板 Chéng

Based on the directions he gave, draw a map showing how to get to the restaurant from school.

Where is the restaurant located? (check all that apply)

- ❑ Between the movie theater and shopping center.
- ❑ In the shopping center.
- ❑ Next to the shopping center.
- ❑ Across the street from the shopping center.
- ❑ Across from the movie theater.
- ❑ Near the movie theater.

When did Xiao Li say she would come to the restaurant?

_____

_____

_____

Working with the Language

用 **and** 把

Before giving directions, the man on the phone said 你用笔记一下。Distinguish the difference between 用 and 把。

Fill in the blanks of the sentences below with either 用 or 把 and then translate each sentence into English.

1. 李文英每天＿＿＿＿筷子吃饭。

_____

2. 因为小李不在家，所以她＿＿＿＿她朋友的电话给陈老板打电话。

_____

3. 小李＿＿＿＿笔画一张地图。

_____

4. 她画完以后，＿＿＿＿地图给她的学生。

_____

5. 小李的学生＿＿＿＿地图找金龙饭店。

_____

6. 陈老板＿＿＿＿菜单给金龙饭店的大师傅。

_____

7. 刘师傅＿＿＿＿很新鲜 (xīnxiān: fresh) 的菜料 (cáiliào: ingredients) 做菜。

_____

8. 菜做好了以后，小姐＿＿＿＿菜放在桌子上。

_____

9. 小李跟她的学生＿＿＿＿现金 (cash) 付帐 (fùzhàng: pay restaurant bill)。

_____

10. 陈老板＿＿＿＿收据 (shōujù: receipt) 给小李。

_____

11. 李文英的学生＿＿＿＿中文给陈老板写信。

_____

12. 陈老板_____这封信贴 (tiē: to stick on) 在饭馆的墙 (qiáng: wall) 上。

_____

* * *

Here are some directions you might give to a friend who is driving or to a taxi cab driver. See if you can translate them into Chinese.

1. Turn left at the shopping center.

_____

2. Turn right after the bookstore.

_____

3. Stop at the third intersection after the movie theater.

_____

4. The Chinese restaurant I'm looking for is across from campus.

_____

* * *

不多久

The man on the phone says, "你不多久会看到我们的饭店." Which sentence(s) is/are closest in conveying the sense of this sentence? (check all that apply)

- ❑ 你很快就可以看到我们的饭店。
- ❑ 你等一下会看到我们的饭店。
- ❑ 你要等很久才会看到我们的饭店。
- ❑ 你马上就看到我们的饭店。

 **Follow-up Activities**

大家来说 **Role-playing (oral)**

One of Xiao Li's students mistakenly left a backpack at the restaurant and had to call Chen Laoban to see if it was there. In enacting this phone conversation, be certain to tell him what color the bag is and what was inside. You will also need to identify yourself, and it might also be nice to thank him for the trouble he went to in arranging the class dinner.

大家来写 Role-playing (written)

Xiao Li's students enjoyed the meal so much that they decided it would be fun to write a note to the owner of the restaurant thanking him for his help and telling him how great the food was. What do you think this letter might say?

_____

_____

_____

_____

_____

_____

_____

_____

_____

Just for fun

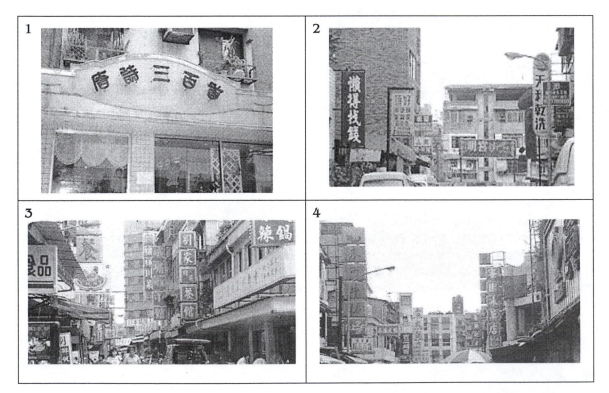

Below are some translations of signs from restaurants in Taipei. See if you can find the sign that is translated. Write the number of the photo in which each 招牌 appears.

	#
Too Lazy to Give Change	
300 Poems of the Tang Dynasty	
Mike's Steaks	
Taiwan University Noodle Shop	
The Liu Family Sichuan Style Restaurant	
The Honey Garden Ices and Fruit Shop	

Lesson 15 第十五课
Birthday Party 生日晚会

Preparation

Identify the following items using the appropriate Chinese characters:

_____ _____ _____

_____ _____ _____

蛋糕 dàngāo   小朋友 "little friends," general term for one or more kids

礼物 lǐwù   面(or miàntiáo 面条)   老人   商场 shāngchǎng

Additional useful vocabulary

订   dìng   V   to order

讲究   jiǎngjiù   Adj   particular about, meticulous, exacting

What do you usually do when you plan a birthday party or when you are invited to attend one? List three things.

_____

_____

_____

_____

_____

_____

_____

_____

_____

_____

What do you think might be some differences between the ways birthdays are celebrated in the United States and in China? List two things. (You might want to look back at your notes from Lesson 3.)

_____

_____

_____

Based on this chart of the Chinese zodiacal signs, answer the following questions

鼠	shǔ	rat		1948; 1960; 1972;1984; 1996
牛	niú	ox, cow		1949; 1961; 1973; 1985; 1997
虎	hǔ	tiger		1950; 1962; 1974; 1986; 1998
兔	tù	rabbit, hare		1951; 1963; 1975;1987; 1999
龙	lóng	dragon		1952; 1964; 1976; 1988; 2000
蛇	shé	snake, serpent		1953; 1965; 1977; 1989; 2001
马	mǎ	horse		1954; 1966; 1978; 1990; 2002

99

羊	yáng	sheep, goat		1955; 1967; 1979; 1991; 2003
猴	hóu	monkey		1956; 1968; 1980; 1992; 2004
鸡	jī	rooster, chicken		1957; 1969; 1981; 1993, 2005
狗	gǒu	dog		1958; 1970; 1982; 1994; 2006
猪	zhū	pig, boar		1959; 1971; 1983; 1995; 2007

你属什么？

如果小李属马，小张属牛， 他们两个大概几岁？

　　　　小李：＿＿＿＿岁

　　　　小张：＿＿＿＿岁

100

 **Listening for the Gist**

Check the topics that Xiao Zhang and Xiao Li mention in this conversation.

    ❑ Whose birthday it is.

    ❑ Age of this person.

    ❑ When and where the birthday party will take place.

    ❑ How many people will attend the party.

    ❑ What activities are planned for the party.

    ❑ What kinds of food will be served.

    ❑ Differences between American and Chinese ways of celebrating birthdays.

    ❑ Other birthday parties they have been to recently.

Where is Zhang Linsheng headed when this conversation takes place?

    ❑ To the market.

    ❑ To school.

    ❑ Returning home.

What does Li Wenying offer to do to help celebrate this birthday?

_____

_____

🔍 Listening for Details

See if you can answer the following questions using pīnyīn or Chinese characters.

Who is having a birthday?

_____

How old is this person?

_____

In what year do you think s/he was born? (You may want to refer to the chart given above.)

_____

Why is Xiao Li surprised to hear that Xiao Zhang is giving a birthday party?

_____

Whose birthday did Xiao Li celebrate when she went to China last year?

_____

How was that birthday celebrated?

_____

How many people were invited?

_____

Why does Xiao Zhang say "你太客气了"?

_____

Check the correct responses based on the conversation.

How many children are invited to the party?

    ❑ More than 10.   ❑ 16.

    ❑ Fewer than 10. ❑ 10.

    ❑ Around 10.

小李要给小张的女儿什么？

    ❑ 毛衣   ❑ 裙子

    ❑ 鞋子   ❑ 帽子

    ❑ 裤子

 **Working with the Language**

订/定

Dìng 订 means to:

reserve   subscribe to   order   make an agreement

Example:

Xiao Zhang says he's going to 订一个蛋糕.

Dìng 定 means to:

determine   set   decide on   make definite

Example:

When Xiao Li goes shopping for a birthday present, the shop owner 已经定了价钱.

Note: Sometimes the meanings overlap and these distinctions are not strictly followed.

How would you translate 订/定 when it takes the following nouns as objects?

_____ 饭馆	_____ 婚	_____ 一件外套
_____ 规矩	_____ 义	_____ 火车票
_____ 合同	_____ 货	_____ 报纸
_____ 牛奶	_____ 日期	_____ 主意
_____ 时间	_____ 杂志	_____ 座位

✳ ✳ ✳

How would you translate Zhang Linsheng's comment "美国人很讲究过生日"?

_____

_____

The expression 讲究 is often used to describe people who are particularly concerned with the precise way things are done, e.g., 穿衣服， 写字， 吃东西， 喝茶，等等. List three more situations (in Chinese) in which someone could be considered 讲究 or 不讲究.

_____   _____   _____

✳ ✳ ✳

A few days later Zhang Linsheng explained to his American friend some of the differences between the ways that Americans and Chinese celebrate birthdays. Complete the following paragraph using these words:

让	得	所以	高兴	不一样
的	碗	最多	很少	
请客	过	讲究	只有	

在美国过生日跟在中国过生日_____。美国人比较_____过生日。在中国_____给孩子过生日，_____吃一_____面条就是了。在中国，_____老人才_____生日。过生日_____人一定要吃面。因为面条很长，_____有长寿(chángshòu: long life) 的意思，_____ 过生日的人觉得很_____。

Now translate this paragraph into idiomatic English.

_____

_____

_____

_____

_____

_____

_____

⇗ Follow-up Activities

 大家来说 Role-playing (oral)

Later that day Li Wenying ran into Xiao Zhang's wife and they talked about the upcoming birthday party. Reenact this conversation with a partner. Be sure to use these words or phrases 过生日，订蛋糕，属，送礼物，吃面条，讲究。

✍ **大家来写 Role-playing (written)**

Last week Xiao Zhang's neighbor had a birthday party for her daughter. Here are some photographs that were taken. Write two sentences describing each photo.

Lesson 16　第十六课
Seeing a Doctor　看病

 Preparation

Rewrite the Chinese characters under the appropriate picture.

_____

_____

_____

_____

_____

_____

_____

_____

_____

瘦	shòu	发烧	fāshāo	住院	zhùyuàn
冷气	lěngqì	咳嗽	késòu	躺	tǎng
感冒	gǎnmào	打针	dǎzhēn		
药	yào	医院	yīyuàn		

Additional useful vocabulary

好几天	hǎo jǐ tiān		many days
一下子	yí xià zi	Adv	all at once
开心		Adj	高兴
特别	tèbié	Adv	especially
严重	yánzhòng	Adj	serious
拖	tuō	V	to delay, to procrastinate

Unfortunately people sometimes get sick when they are traveling. List some reasons why this might occur. Have you ever had this kind of experience? If so, describe what happened.

Since the opposite of 外 is 内 (nèi), what do you think 国内 and 国外 mean?

_____

In this dialogue 国内 refers to _____ and 国外 refers to _____.

倒 dào, on the contrary, shows the opposite of what was expected.

Examples:

妹妹十岁，姐姐十四岁，妹妹倒比姐姐高。

Older sister is 10 and younger sister 14, but (much to our surprise) younger sister is taller than older sister.

她住得最近，倒来得最晚。

She lives the closest but it turns out that she arrived latest.

How would you translate this sentence?

沒看医生，她的病倒好了。

_____

_____

＊　＊　＊

一会儿 A，一会儿 B。

One minute this, one minute that.

Example: How would you translate this sentence?

他一会儿要看电影，一会儿要去跳舞，就是不要在家里看书。

_____

_____

反正　　fǎnzhèng　　anyway, in any case

Examples: How would you translate these sentences?

我可以送你回家，反正我家离你家很近。

_____

_____

他买不买还不一定，反正我要买。

_____

_____

108

 # Listening for the Gist

Where did Xiao Li just return from?

❑ Changchun.   ❑ Nanjing.

❑ Beijing.   ❑ Shanghai.

Was she sick in China or did she fall ill after she returned?

_____

Check all the topics Xiao Li and Xiao Zhang mentioned in this conversation.

	✓
Her symptoms when she first didn't feel well.	
Taking over-the-counter cold medicine.	
Drinking herbal tea.	
Staying in bed all day.	
Going to the hospital.	
Getting shots.	
Her family's concern for her health.	

 # Listening for Details

What were Li Wenying's symptoms?

❑ Fever.   ❑ Muscle soreness.

❑ Diarrhea.   ❑ Sneezing.

❑ Cough.   ❑ Fatigue.

❑ Headache.

How long was she in the hospital?

❑ 2 days.   ❑ 3 days.

❑ 4 days.   ❑ A week.

Based on this experience, what does she resolve to do in the future? (check all that apply)

❑ 不能拖   ❑ 要把冷气关掉

❑ 要多吃感冒药   ❑ 一发烧就要躺下来

❑ 一生病就得去看医生   ❑ 要多注意身体

Working with the Language

Listen carefully to the beginning of the conversation, paying special attention to these lines:

张：怎么你一下子瘦了那么多啊！我看你是不是在国内玩得太累了？

李：那倒不是，在国内玩得挺开心，但是就是我病了一个多星期。

Translate into English what Xiao Zhang said, paying special attention to the uses of de 得.

_____

_____

_____

Explain the function of the 倒 in Xiao Li's response.

_____

_____

Now go back and underline the descriptive complements (or resultative clauses) introduced by 得.

Complete the following sentences. Remember that what comes after 得 shows a comment on or the result of the verb.

1. 小李病得_____。

2. 小李的丈夫著急得_____。

3. 那个星期小李药吃得_____。

4. 医院的医生忙得_____。

5. 过了一个星期小李就累得_____。

In this conversation Xiao Li said that she 不能不去医院. How would you translate her statement?

_____

_____

Chinese frequently uses double negatives. Circle the negatives in the following paragraph. Then translate the paragraph into idiomatic English.

小李刚回家的时候没觉得不舒服。可是过了几天， 她就又咳嗽又发烧了。丈夫劝 (quàn: to advise) 小李去看病， 可是到了医院以后才发现那儿的医生沒有一个不忙。小李知道她这么不舒服，非等不可 (i.e., 不能不等)。过了一个半小时，医生才给她看病，告诉小李感冒的时候不能不在家休息。再说， 她不可以不吃药。医生还提醒 （tíxǐng: to remind）她，一个人不能不注意自己的身体，沒有人不愿意健康 (jiànkāng: healthy)。小李心里想，她如果不听医生的话，就好不了 (hǎobuliǎo: won't get better) 了。她家里的人也都同意，而且很高兴小李沒得 （dé: to get) 什么治不了(zhì-buliǎo: cannot be cured, incurable) 的病。

_____

_____

_____

_____

_____

_____

_____

_____

_____

_____

_____

_____

_____

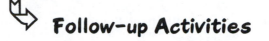 **Follow-up Activities**

 大家来说 **Role-playing (oral)**

With a partner, imagine the conversation that took place when Li Wenying went to the hospital in China. It turned out that the doctor she saw was a friend of her parents, and in fact this doctor's son was also studying in graduate school in the U.S. So they had a lot to talk about in addition to Li Wenying's health problems. Be sure to include the following vocabulary: 不舒服，特别，其实，躺，反正，怪不得，严重，拖，好几天，身体，健康, verb +得+ descriptive complement.

Reading

A few weeks later Xiao Li's uncle fell ill. Below is a prescription he was given. Complete this chart based on the information in the prescription.

Patient's name	
Age	
Patient's medical history number	
Date prescription was written	
Name of hospital that filled the prescription	
How high should patient's temperature be before he takes aspirin?*	
How often should he take aspirin?	
How often should he take the second medicine that is prescribed?	
Doctor's family name	

*__Note:__ Remember, it's given in Celsius not Fahrenheit.

宏恩綜合醫院

處 方 箋

病歷號 71489

住院號 _____

姓名 王天竟　年齡 48　性別 男　處方號 _____

R

2000 年 6 月 21 日

1, 阿司匹靈 0.3×12

　服法：體溫超過攝氏三十八度

　　　　時每四至六小時服一粒

2, 紅黴素 0.5×12

　服法：每六小時服一丸

醫師 李逐(公)　配方藥師 _____　校正藥師 _____

Lesson 17 第十七课
Dating 約会

 **Preparation**

Useful vocabulary

单独	dāndú	Adj/Adv	alone, individually, on one's own
周年	zhōunían	N	anniversary
说来就长	shuōlái jiù cháng	Coll	it's a long story (also 说來话长)
单位	dānwèi	N	unit (in an organization or administration)
编辑	biānjí	N	editor
夫妇	fūfù	N	couple, husband and wife
丈夫	zhàngfu	N	husband (also 先生)
庆祝	qìngzhù	V	to celebrate
左右	zuǒyòu	Suf	approximately

Listening for the Gist

Why did Zhang Linsheng call Li Wenying?

  ❑   He wants her to babysit.

  ❑   He wants her to join him and his wife for dinner and a movie.

  ❑   He wants advice about buying an anniversary present for his wife.

  ❑   He wants to invite her over tomorrow night for dinner.

How long have Zhang Linsheng and his wife been married?

  ❑   8 years.   ❑   11 years.

  ❑   10 years.   ❑   12 years.

How did they first meet?

_____

_____

_____

🔍 Listening for Details

What day of the week is it?

☐ Thursday.   ☐ Saturday.

☐ Friday.   ☐ Sunday.

What kind of jobs did Zhang Linsheng and his wife have when they first met?

_____

_____

_____

What prompted them to start dating?

_____

_____

How long did they date before they got married?

☐ Six months.   ☐ Two years.

☐ One year.   ☐ Three years.

What time does Xiao Zhang want Xiao Li to come to their house?

☐ 5:30.   ☐ 6:30.

☐ 6:00.   ☐ 7:00.

What time do they plan to return?

☐ 10:00.   ☐ 11:00.

☐ 10:30.   ☐ 12:00.

📘 Working with the Language

Write the pīnyīn for the measure words or classifiers (量词 liàngcí) Xiao Zhang uses for these nouns.

_____电影   _____饭

What 量词 should be used with these objects?

封	张	棵 kē	辆 liàng	条
把	座 zuò	朵 duǒ	付	所

In Chinese some words, known as 破音字 pòyīnzì or 多音字 duōyīnzì, have more than one pronunciation, depending on the meaning. For example, kàn usually means to read, but when it's pronounced in the first tone it means to look after, to watch (remember Xiao Zhang asks Xiao Li to kān háizi 看孩子).

Here are some other common words that are sometimes pronounced in different tones. The pinyin for each pronunciation and examples of compounds with each pronunciation are given in this chart. Complete the chart. The first entry has been done for you.

Character	Pīnyīn	Compounds	Pīnyīn	English
假	jiǎ	假如	jiǎrú	if
	jià	放假		
好	hǎo	很好		
	hào	爱好		
教	jiāo	教书		
	jiào	佛教	fójiào	
乐	lè	快乐		
	yuè	音乐		
长	cháng	长城	chángchéng	
	zhǎng	长大		
少	shǎo	多少		
	shào	少年		young adults, juvenile
得	dé	跑得快		
	děi	得上课		
大	dà	长大		
	dài	大夫	dàifu	
分	fēn	一分钱，分开		
	fèn	身分		
重	zhòng	重要		
	chóng	重写		

Character	Pīnyīn	Compounds	Pīnyīn	English
差	chā	差不多		
	chà	差		
	chāi	出差		to go on a business trip
种	zhǒng	各种		
	zhòng	种菜		
论	lùn	讨论	tǎolùn	
	lún	论语		
觉	jué	觉得		
	jiào	睡觉		
要	yào	要是		
	yaò	重要		
	yào	要面子		
	yāo	要求	yāoqiú	
看	kàn	看法		
	kān	看家		

Complete these sentences using the appropriate pòyīnzì/duōyīnzì chosen from the preceding table. Write the Chinese characters and pīnyīn. Then translate each sentence into English.

1. 张林生和他太太还沒结婚的时候，常常听_____。因为这是他们的_____。

2. _____李文英要六点钟_____张林生的女儿，她_____五点四十_____ 离开她的家。

3. 小李到张家的时候，张太太正在_____菜。她女儿在她房间_____。

118

4. 小张的女儿喜欢留 (liú: to [let] grow)_____头发 (tóufa, tóufǎ): hair)，可是她妈妈 _____这样不好 _____。

5. 小李的学生对印度 (Yìndu: India) 很有兴趣。他们的_____请了一个老师_____佛_____(Buddhism) 的课。他们非常_____。

6. 小李也告诉她的学生_____是一本很_____的书。_____每个中国学生都知道这本书。

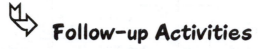

Follow-up Activities

大家来说 **Role-playing (oral)**

The way that Xiao Zhang and his wife dated before they got married is fairly typical for many Chinese students. What are some ways that their experience differs from dating practices in the U.S.? With a partner discuss the strengths and weaknesses of each system. Be sure to use some of these words and expressions:

同学　对象　朋友　一起　左右　认识　出去　跳舞　周末

大家来写 **Role-playing (written)**

Create a dialogue in Chinese based on this picture. First provide some background information, such as the names of the people who speak, where and when the conversation takes place, and a sentence saying how well they know each other.

_____

_____

_____

_____

_____

_____

_____

Lesson 18 第十八课
Renting an Apartment 租房子

 **Preparation**

Useful vocabulary

签证	qiānzhèng	N	visa
换	huàn	V	to change
合适	héshì	Adj	suitable
搬家	bānjiā	V	to move
包括	bāokuò	V	to include

If you were looking for an apartment (gōngyù 公寓), what would matter most to you? Rank in order of importance, one (1) being highest.

_____ location 地点

_____ deposit 押金 (yājīn)

_____ size of living room 客厅

_____ number of units in building

_____ number of bathrooms 洗澡间

_____ number of bedrooms 卧室

_____ cost of rent 房租

_____ cost of utilities 水电费

_____ term of contract 租约期限 (zūyuē qíxiàn or qíxiàn)

_____ type of landlord 房东

_____ availability of parking 车位

_____ convenience of public transportation 交通

120

 # Listening for the Gist

Why is Li Wenying looking for an apartment?

_____

_____

How does Zhang Linsheng think he can help her?

_____

_____

Listening for Details

What does Xiao Li mention regarding her apartment hunting? (check all that apply)

- ❏ location
- ❏ amenities
- ❏ deposit
- ❏ size of living room
- ❏ number of units in building
- ❏ number of bathrooms

- ❏ number of bedrooms
- ❏ cost of rent
- ❏ cost of utilities
- ❏ term of contract
- ❏ type of landlord
- ❏ availability of parking

Complete the chart based on the information Zhang Linsheng gives about his friend.

name	
telephone number	
location of apartment	
size of apartment	
cost of rent	
cost of utilities	
when the apt will be available	

When does Xiao Li say she will call Xiao Zhang's friend?

- ❏ Right away.
- ❏ This afternoon.
- ❏ Tonight.
- ❏ Tomorrow morning.
- ❏ After she talks to her husband.

 **Working with the Language**

verb + 得/不 + 下 Potential Complements

Toward the beginning of this conversation Xiao Li makes the following comment: 以前我住在一个一个卧室的公寓里。他们来了就住不下了. How would you translate her statement? (Hint: 住不下 means "won't be able to live there any longer.")

_____

_____

Complete these sentences using one of the following verbs plus either 得下 or 不下, depending on the context. Some verbs may be used more than once.

吃　　喝　　住　　坐　　放

1. 那个电影院很小，恐怕_____一百多人。

2. 虽然他们家很小，可是书架很多，张林生刚买的书一定_____。

3. 我们一边聊天一边喝茶，已经喝了两三个小时，我真_____了。

4. 这个教室非常大，两百个人也_____。

5. 小李现在住的公寓不太大，她先生跟女儿来了以后，三个人就_____。

6. 小张上个星期六做了很多菜，像红烧牛肉，麻婆豆腐，宫爆鸡，等等，最后还有一条很大的清蒸鱼。他的太太跟女儿都_____了。

＊　　＊　　＊

连 ... 都（也）...

Xiao Zhang says that the apartment he knows about has this advantage: 连水电都包括. How would you translate his comment?

_____

_____

Based on the information in each of the following sentences, write a sentence using 连 …
都（也）…

Example:

本来小李的先生去年想来美国，可是她沒申请 (shēnqǐng：to apply for) 签证。

↳ 小李的先生去年连签证都沒有申请。

1. 小李上个月天天找房子。下雪的时候她还去看了。

_____

2. 小李也打了很多电话。

_____

3. 小李觉得找房子很累。他沒时间吃饭。

_____

4. 这几天天气特别冷，小李又沒穿毛衣，也沒戴帽子，怪不得她感冒了。

_____

5. 小李感冒的时候完全不愿意吃药。

_____

⇩ Follow-up Activities

Xiao Li called Zhang Linsheng's friend to find out more about the apartment. Before she called she made a list of some additional things she wanted to ask about. In addition to things from the list above, she also wanted to ask if there's a playground or park nearby, what type of people live in the building, whether the building is noisy or if there is a lot of street noise, how close the apartment is to pre-schools or daycare centers. Write this list in Chinese.

_____   _____

_____   _____

_____   _____

_____   _____

大家来说 Role-playing (oral)

Now enact this conversation with a partner.

Reading

Here is an ad from a Chinese newspaper. Answer the questions based on this ad.

Where do you think this newspaper is published? Why?

_____

What is the telephone number of the apartment for rent on Linsen 林森 North Rd.?

_____

Find the ad for the apartment on Da'an 大安路 Rd. What does it say about transportation?

_____

Circle the rental properties that advertise furnished apartments.

_____

Which property is close to the airport? Which property is near the train station?

_____

Which ads are for business office space?

_____

Lesson 19 第十九课
Post Office 邮局

 **Preparation**

Useful vocabulary

Identify the following items using the appropriate Chinese characters:

明信片	míngxìnpiàn	邮件	yóujiàn
邮票	yóupiào	盒子	hézi
包裹	bāoguǒ	信封	xìnfēng

Verbs 动词

寄	jì	to send
邮	yóu	to mail
装	zhuāng	to pack
运	yùn	to transport (海运 hǎiyùn, 空运 kōngyùn)
省	shěng	to save (省钱，省事 to save trouble, to simplify matters)
收	shōu	to receive
贴	tiē	to affix, to paste

Listening for the Gist

What was Zhang Linsheng doing at the post office?

_____

What was Li Wenying doing at the post office?

_____

Listening for Details

Why does Xiao Li say "恭喜恭喜"?

- ❑ It's New Year's.
- ❑ Zhang Linsheng is about to graduate.
- ❑ Zhang Linsheng got a job in the U.S.
- ❑ Zhang Linsheng got a job in China.

Which of the following items does Zhang Linsheng say he is mailing?

- ❑ Books.
- ❑ Clothes.
- ❑ Toys.
- ❑ Television.
- ❑ Radio.
- ❑ Computer.
- ❑ CD player.

How long does Zhang Linsheng think it will take to mail packages by sea mail to China?

- ❑ Three weeks.
- ❑ One month.
- ❑ Two months.
- ❑ Three months.
- ❑ Four months.

Based on the conversation, circle whether the following statements about Lin Wenying are true (是) or false (非).

她不知道张林生快要毕业了。	是	非
她看到了一个装玩具的盒子。	是	非
她要买邮票。	是	非
她要寄包裹。	是	非
她要买明信片。	是	非
她要把明信片寄到中国。	是	非
她要把明信片寄到美国。	是	非
她要给她母亲写信。	是	非
她现在不忙，可以帮小张的忙。	是	非
她现在很忙，沒时间帮小张的忙。	是	非

Working with the Language

How would you translate:

国际   guójí   国内   guónèi   国外   guówài

_____

In this dialogue, which countries are referred to as 国内 and 国外?

国内 = _____

国外 = _____

Modification with de 的

Below are some phrases with de. Write a complete sentence with each phrase, then translate the entire sentence.

Example:

装玩具的盒子

↳ 张林生要把装玩具的盒子寄到中国。

Zhang Linsheng is going to mail the box packed with toys to China.

1. 寄回去的衣服

_____

2. 在美国买的电脑

_____

3. 冬天戴的帽子

_____

4. 在中国找到的工作

_____

5. 贴在信封上的邮票

_____

6. 在邮局见面的同学

_____

7. 邮海运的英文书跟中文书

_____

8. 前年在购物中心买的电视

_____

9. 寄给朋友的明信片

_____

10. 寄给住在国内的朋友的明信片

_____

至少　　　zhìshǎo　　　　at least

Answer the questions using zhìshǎo.

Example:

寄海运慢不慢?

↳　很慢,至少要等三个月才到。

1. 小张要寄几个盒子?

_____

2. 小李要买几张邮票?

_____

3. 小张的太太衣服多不多?

_____

4. 那天邮局的人多不多?

_____

5. 你认为把电脑寄到中国贵不贵?

_____

Follow-up Activities

大家来说 **Role-playing (oral)**

After waiting in line for 15 minutes, Zhang Linsheng is assisted by a postal worker who helps him decide the best way to mail his packages. He has to tell the worker what is in each box and whether he wants to send it air mail or sea mail. He asks when the boxes will probably arrive and how much it will cost to buy additional insurance. The postal worker tells him the cost of each package and asks him if he wants a receipt. With a partner enact this conversation. The postal worker's first question is given below:

这个盒子里装的是什么?

_____

_____

_____

_____

_____

_____

_____

_____

✍ 大家来写 Role-playing (written)

Meanwhile Li Wenying is at another counter buying stamps. Complete the conversation she is having with this postal worker:

李：　　　请问，你们这儿卖邮票吗?

营业员：　_____。你要买什么样的_____?

李：　　　_____。

营业员：　这些明信片你要寄到哪儿?

李：　　　_____。

营业员：　你有几封信要寄?

李：　　　_____。

营业员：　要寄到哪儿?

李：　　　_____。

营业员：　寄到_____每张要_____钱，你要几张?

李：　　　_____。

营业员：　那一共要_____块钱。你要不要一个收据?

李： ＿＿＿＿＿＿＿＿＿＿＿＿＿＿＿＿＿。

营业员： 好，给你了。

李： 谢谢。

营业员： ＿＿＿＿＿＿＿＿＿＿＿＿＿＿＿＿＿。

Reading

Below is a communication from the post office. What is the point of this notice?

國內
國際快捷郵件候投通知單

茲有由 ＵＩＤ

局寄交 台端第 _____ 號國內

件 件，業經投遞一次，無法妥投。下次將於 6 月

16 日 P12 時左右到達 貴處投遞，敬請 屆時留府

候領，以便妥投。

此 致

先生
女士

李文英

台灣北區郵政管理局快捷郵件股
台北市愛國東路246號3樓
國內快捷郵件：三九七〇三五五一七
電話：國際快捷郵件：三五六八〇八七
１０６０５

業務士 章

71 年 6 月 日

1. When was the notice written?

_____

2. When will the post office attempt delivery again?

_____

3. How many items of mail are to be delivered?

_____

4. Is the mail international or national?

_____

5. Translate the complete address of the post office into English.

_____

6. What number should one call for further information about this delivery?

_____

Lesson 20 第二十课
On Sports 运动

 Preparation

Identify these sports using the appropriate Chinese characters:

_____   _____   _____

_____   _____   _____

_____   _____   _____

_____   _____   _____

踢足球	滑雪 huáxuě	溜冰 liūbīng
游泳	打棒球 bàngqiú	打篮球
打网球	练太极拳 liàn táijíquán	打乒乓球
跑步	练剑术 jiànshù	橄榄球 gǎnlǎnqiú (=美式足球)

满头大汗

How would you translate this expression?

_____

 Listening for the Gist

What is the main sport mentioned?

❑ football ❑ basketball

❑ soccer ❑ running

Who plays this/these sport(s)?

	played this sport in the past	plays this sport in the present
张林生		
李文英		
张林生和李文英		

Listening for Details

Who does Xiao Zhang play this sport with?

- ❑ Only Chinese men.
- ❑ Mostly Chinese men and women.
- ❑ Only American men.
- ❑ Mostly American men and women.

What is Xiao Li worried will happen if she plays this sport?

- ❑ She will be hurt.
- ❑ She will be embarrassed.
- ❑ She will not be as good as other players.
- ❑ She will be the only female player.
- ❑ Other players will laugh at her.

What does Xiao Zhang say to reassure Xiao Li that she is welcome to join him and his teammates? (check all that apply)

- ❑ 没事了!
- ❑ 没系关!
- ❑ 没问题啊!
- ❑ 我们欢迎你参加!
- ❑ 不会的!
- ❑ 不要担心啊!

How often does Xiao Zhang play this sport?

_____

When did Xiao Li play this sport?

- ❑ In middle school.
- ❑ In high school.
- ❑ In college.
- ❑ After she graduated from college.

 **Working with the Language**

A. Arrange the sentences in the order they are spoken in the dialogue and circle who the speaker is.

_____我们星期六的下午三点开始踢。　　　　小张　小李

_____那到时候我们一起去吧!　　　　　　　小张　小李

_____一般踢一个半小时。　　　　　　　　小张　小李

_____刚跑步啊!　　　　　　　　　　　　小张　小李

_____我已经有三年没踢足球了。　　　　　小张　小李

_____我们一个星期一定要踢一次足球。　　小张　小李

B. Go back and circle all the time words or expressions in these sentences. Note whether they indicate duration of time, approximate time or precise time.

C. Now translate each sentence, making sure you use the appropriate verb tense based on the information about time that is given.

_____

_____

_____

_____

_____

_____

_____

_____

＊　＊　＊

这么… 还 …

Toward the beginning of the conversation Xiao Li says,

"这么热的天气还踢足球？"

How would you translate this sentence? (hint: there is more than one correct answer)

- ❑ Even though it is so hot you still play soccer!
- ❑ How can you play soccer in such hot weather?
- ❑ How hot was the weather when you played soccer?
- ❑ Even you play soccer in such hot weather?
- ❑ Will you still play soccer if the weather is this hot?
- ❑ Why would anyone play soccer in such hot weather?

Translate each sentence into Chinese using 这么…还… (Hint: Xiao Li could also have said 天气这么热还踢足球 and it would have meant the same thing.)

1. Even though those tennis shoes are so expensive Xiao Li still wants to buy them.

_____

2. Xiao Li's roommate even goes jogging when there is so much traffic.

_____

3. The swimming pool is so far away but many students still swim there every day.

_____

4. Xiao Zhang's American friend plays basketball outside even in such cold weather.

_____

5. Taijiquan is so complicated (fùzá 复杂) yet a lot of people practice it often.

_____

6. Even though there are so few people, they still want to play baseball.

_____

 # Follow-up Activities

大家来说 **Role-playing (oral)**

Recently Li Wenying's friend sent her some pictures of a qigong class she is taking in China. With a partner describe what you see in these qigong exercise classes.

大家来写 **Role-playing (written)**

Write a paragraph about a sport or activity you enjoy. Be sure to tell when you …

      played a sport for a specific amount of time.

      just recently played a sport.

      played a sport a certain number of times per week or month.

      played a sport at an exactly specified time.

      plan to play a sport in the future at an approximate time.

      haven't played a sport in a certain amount of time.

_____

_____

_____

_____

_____

_____

_____

_____

_____

_____

_____

_____

_____

_____

_____

_____

Lesson 21 第二十一课
Travel 旅行

 **Preparation**

Useful vocabulary

打算	dǎsuàn	V	to plan
旅遊	lǚyóu	V	to travel (cf. 旅行)
加州	Jiāzhōu	N	California
打折	dǎzhé	V	to give a discount
而且	érqiě	Conj	furthermore, moreover

Can you figure out what U.S. cities these are? Try to guess by sound or meaning.

芝加哥 _____   丹佛 _____   波士顿 _____

西雅图 _____   小石城 _____   迈阿密 _____

洛杉矶 _____   达拉斯 _____   华盛顿 _____

If you were recommending places that foreign students should visit while they are living in the States, which of these would you recommend and why?

Smithsonian Museum	斯密生博物馆 (Sīmìshēng bówùguǎn)
Statue of Liberty	自由女神像 (Zìyóunǚ shén xiàng)
Disneyland	迪斯尼乐园 (Dísīní lèyuán)
Liberty Bell	自由钟
Yellowstone National Park	黄石公园
Rocky Mountain Park	落矶山脉 (Luòjīshānmài)
Grand Canyon	大峡谷 (Dàxiágǔ)
The U.S. Capitol	美国国会大厦 (xià)

140

What other places might you suggest? Why?

_____

_____

_____

Indicate which of the following terms you think refer to men and which refer to women. Then write the letter of the definition for these general family terms. (**Note:** Keep in mind that sometimes other factors such as regional differences and distinctions in age or marital status may affect the terms used for certain family members.) Several entries have already been done for you.

男 女	_c_ 舅舅 jiùjiu	a. 母亲的姐妹
男 女	_a_ 阿姨 āyí	b. 舅舅的母亲
男 女	___ 姑姑 gūgu	c. 母亲的哥哥弟弟
男 女	_f_ 叔叔 shūshu	d. 父亲的姐妹
男 女	___ 伯伯 bóbo	e. 舅舅的太太
男 女	___ 舅妈 jiùma	f. 父亲的弟弟
男 女	___ 外婆 wàipó	g. 父亲的哥哥

 Listening for the Gist

The main topic of this conversation is:

- ❑ Xiao Zhang's plans for a family vacation.
- ❑ The cost of traveling in the United States.
- ❑ Historical places in the U.S. Xiao Zhang and his family should visit before they return to China.
- ❑ Whether Xiao Zhang and his family should drive or fly on their vacation.
- ❑ Where Li Wenying has relatives living in the U.S.

What kinds of suggestions does Li Wenying make?

_____

_____

_____

_____

Listening for Details

How much was Xiao Zhang planning to spend on airfare?

_____

_____

How much are the tickets Xiao Li knows about?

_____

_____

他们家为什么要去加州？

- ❑ 要看李文英的舅舅和舅妈。
- ❑ 要省钱。
- ❑ 小张的女儿沒去过迪斯尼乐园。
- ❑ 小张沒时间带她女儿去玩。
- ❑ 小张觉得加州的天气最好。

李文英为什么提到她的舅舅？ (check all that apply)

- ❑ 他住在洛杉矶。
- ❑ 小张的女儿可以跟他们家的孩子玩。
- ❑ 他家离迪斯尼乐园非常近。
- ❑ 张林生可以住在他家。
- ❑ 小李要请小张把东西交给他。
- ❑ 他可以帮小张的忙。

Working with the Language

掉 diào

The basic meaning of 掉 is to fall, to drop down.

Examples:

我每次看那个电影都掉眼泪。 (yǎnlèi: tears)

到了冬天树叶子都掉了。 (yèzi: leaves)

掉 + 在 means to fall or drop to a certain place.

Examples:

书掉在地下。

那个小孩的手套掉在路上。(shǒutáo: gloves)

掉 can also mean to omit, to lack.

Example:

这句话掉了一个字。

Verb + 掉 + 了 (resultative complement) indicates that the action of the verb has been accomplished.

In this conversation Zhang Linsheng said "我的汽车已经卖掉了." Complete these sentences using one of the verbs given below + 掉. Then translate each sentence into English.

忘　　　吃　　　坏　　　卖　　　跑　　　走

1. 小李本来要五点钟给她舅舅打电话，可是她_____了。

_____

_____

2. 张林生的女儿跟她的小朋友把蛋糕都_____了。

_____

_____

3. 小张要买很便宜的飞机票，可是他听说那种票早就_____了。

_____

_____

4. 李文英打算做麻婆豆腐，可是豆腐已经_____了。

_____

_____

5. 昨天小张找买他汽车的人，可是他_____了。

_____

_____

Interrogative words are sometimes used in an indefinite sense to mean "which ever one," "whatever," "wherever," etc. When Xiao Li asks Xiao Zhang: "有沒有决定坐哪家航空公司？" he responds by saying: "哪家航空公司便宜就坐哪家." How would you translate his response?

_____

_____

Answer these questions using interrogative words in each case. In some instances you are given hints in parentheses.

1. 他们打算买哪天的飞机票？

_____

2. 坐飞机的时候他们要坐哪儿？（位子，空）

_____

3. 他们要在迪斯尼乐园看什么？（有意思）

_____

4. 他们在加州的时候要吃什么样的饭？（方便）

_____

⤵ Follow-up Activities

大家来说 Role-playing (oral)

After talking it over with his family and getting the flight information from Xiao Li, Xiao Zhang decided to call a travel agent to help him book the best and cheapest flight. With a partner enact this conversation.

大家来写 Role-playing (written)

It's not surprising that Zhang Linsheng's daughter wants to go to Disneyland. Disney products and movies are well advertised and readily available in many parts of China and Taiwan. Recently Zhang Linsheng's friend sent him a photograph of a new shopping district in Suzhou (located near a famous temple). Imagine you are going to interview five of the people in the area about their attitudes toward having a Disney store right there and the impact this has on Chinese culture.

Write your questions in Chinese here:

1._____

_____

2._____

_____

3._____

_____

4._____

_____

5._____

_____

Lesson 22 第二十二课
Hometown 家乡

 **Preparation**

Useful vocabulary

Identify the following pictures using the appropriate Chinese characters:

_____   _____   _____

_____   _____

盖房子　　gài fángzi　　　拆房子　　　chāi fángzi　　　到处都是人

高楼　　　gāolóu　　　　交通很乱　　luàn（塞车 sāichē）

Additional useful vocabulary

变化　biànhuà　　　　N　　　change(s)

到处　dàochù　　　　Adv　　everywhere

想像　xiǎngxiàng　　　V/N　　to imagine, imagination

干净	gānjìng	Adj	clean (opposite 脏 zāng: dirty)
气候	qìhòu	N	weather, climate
爱	ài	V	to love, to be fond of (opposite 恨 hèn: to hate)
污染	wūrǎn	V/N	to pollute, pollution (空气污染 kōngqìwūrǎn: air pollution)

 **Listening for the Gist**

Who is from originally from Beijing? (circle one)

李文英   张林生

Who just returned from Beijing? (circle one)

李文英   张林生

What are some of the changes in Beijing that are mentioned in this conversation? (check all that apply)

- ❑ More pollution.
- ❑ Increase in traffic.
- ❑ More new construction.
- ❑ Higher standard of living.
- ❑ More people have cars.
- ❑ More high rise buildings.
- ❑ Greater unemployment.
- ❑ More restaurants.
- ❑ Worse weather.

Listening for Details

How long has it been since Zhang Linsheng was in Beijing?

_____

_____

What season does he remember as having the best weather?

- ❑ 夏天
- ❑ 冬天
- ❑ 秋天
- ❑ 春天

Write in pīnyīn and/or Chinese characters the two comments Xiao Li makes about the weather.

1. _____

_____

2. _____

_____

 **Working with the Language**

When Li Wenying's parents asked her about her studies in the U.S., here's what she said: "Studying Chinese literature in America is really different from what I imagined." How would you translate her response into Chinese? (Remember Zhang Linsheng's comment about Beijing? He said "跟我想像的北京可不太一样了.")

_____

_____

Using the phrase "到处都是 …," describe the following places:

北京的火车站

_____

香港的购物中心

_____

迪斯尼乐园

_____

北京大学的图书馆

_____

上海的饭馆

_____

台北的动物园

_____

148

Draw lines connecting the antonyms 连连看.

原来	恨
盖	冷
干净	平房
热	拆
高楼	脏
爱	现在

Write a complete sentence in the spaces provided below using a subject + verb + resultative 得 from Column A and the result from Column B. Then translate each sentence into English. The first sentence has been done for you.

Column A	Column B
李文英热得	不敢出门
交通乱得	非常厉害
高楼盖得	谁都不高兴
空气污染厉害得	连公共汽车也不能走
天气冷得	满头大旱
车子塞得	应该多穿一点衣服
小李热得	越多越好

Example:

1. 李文英热得不敢出门.

Li Wenying was so hot she wouldn't dare go outside.

2._____

3._____

4._____

5._____

6._____

7._____

 **Follow-up Activities**

大家来说 **Role-playing (oral)**

That evening Xiao Zhang and his wife talked about the way that Beijing has changed. His wife Liu Zhen 刘珍 is from a small town in the countryside in Hunan. According to her, things haven't really changed there that much. Below are some pictures of the area around her hometown. With a partner create a conversation based on these photos.

大家来写 **Role-playing (written)**

What do you think are some reasons why China has changed so much in the past ten years? Write a short paragraph in which you discuss at least three of these factors.

_____

_____

_____

_____

_____

_____

_____

Lesson 23　第二十三课
At the Airport　在机场

 Preparation

Useful vocabulary

Identify the following items using the appropriate Chinese characters:

TO:　Liwenying@colorado.uscu

FROM:　Zhanglinsheng@hotmail.com

RE:　wǒ dàole

_____

_____

_____

_____

电子邮件	传真机	chuánzhēnjī
文件	护照	hùzhào
机票	签证	qiānzhèng

＊　＊　＊

Additional useful vocabulary

道别	dàobié	V O	to say goodbye (formal; implies a separation of a long time)
超重	chāozhòng	V	to exceed the weight limit
检查	jiǎnchá	V	to examine

换钱	huànqián	V	to change money
保持	bǎochí	V	to maintain, to keep
联系	liánxì	V/N	to maintain contact; to connect (cf.联络 liánluò: to contact); contact, connection

When is it appropriate to say: 祝你一路顺风?

_____

_____

_____

What arrangements do you need to make ahead of time if you are planning to fly to China or Taiwan?

_____

_____

_____

What do you need to do when you get to the airport?

_____

_____

_____

Listening for the Gist

Why does Zhang Linsheng call Li Wenying?
- ❏ To ask her to take him and his family to the airport.
- ❏ To ask her advise about what time they should be at the airport.
- ❏ To ask her how much baggage is allowed on international flights.
- ❏ To say goodbye.

What else do they talk about?

_____

_____

_____

_____

_____

152

Listening for Details

Based on this conversation, complete this chart.

Day of departure.	
Time plane departs.	
Time they plan to arrive at the airport.	
Time they will leave for the airport.	

小李提醒小张到了中国以后

- ❑ 给她打電話
- ❑ 给她寄电子邮件
- ❑ 给她写一封信
- ❑ 给她发传真

Based on what Zhang Linsheng says, complete this sentence and translate it into English:

一般来说_____

_____

_____

 Working with the Language

Draw lines connecting the antonyms 连连看

接   回家
寄   见面
分开   忘记
道别   高兴
记得   送
出门   受
难过   欢迎

✳ ✳ ✳

Check the best definition for 联络

- ☐ 有来往
- ☐ 聊天
- ☐ 旅遊
- ☐ 庆祝

* * *

一定不要 （别）Strong Prohibitive Definitely don't + verb

In this conversation Xiao Li reminded Xiao Zhang to make sure his family's luggage didn't exceed the weight allowed by the airlines.* When Xiao Zhang called his landlord to say goodbye, he was given a lot of travel advice by him too. Translate these concerns into Chinese:

Definitely do not …

… take too much luggage.

_____

… put a pocketknife （小刀）in your suitcase.

_____

… forget to bring some snacks to eat during the flight.

_____

… get to the airport too late.

_____

… forget to bring your passport and plane ticket.

_____

… take fruit into a foreign country.

_____

… forget to change money before you get on the plane.

_____

… smoke（抽烟 chōuyān） on the plane.

_____

Note: Xiao Li said "一定不要把行李超重," but a more standard way of saying this is "一定不要让行李超重."

154

Follow-up Activities

大家来写 **Role-playing (written)**

Before landing in Beijing, Xiao Zhang was given this customs form to fill out. Can you fill it out for him?

A few days after Zhang Linsheng and his family arrived in Beijing he sent Li Wenying an email. In this message he talked about the flight, his impressions of Beijing, and what he has been doing since he returned to China. He also asked about what she's been doing. Imagine you are Zhang Linsheng and write this email message for him.

TO: Liwenying@colorado.uscu

FROM: Zhanglinsheng@hotmail.com

RE: wǒ dàole

_____

_____

_____

_____

_____

_____

 大家來说 **Role-playing (oral)**

After Lin Wenying received this email she called another classmate to talk about how Zhang Linsheng was doing. With a partner enact this conversation.

Lesson 24 (CD2.1) 第二十四课
Going to the Market 上市场买菜

 Preparation

Rewrite the Chinese characters under the appropriate picture.

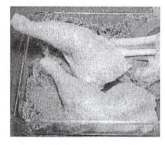

_____

_____

_____

_____

_____

_____

_____

_____

海虾	hǎixiā	牛肉	niúròu	鱼	yú
啤酒	píjiǔ	生菜	shēngcài	鸡腿	jītuǐ
菊花	júhuā	玫瑰花	méiguīhuā	西红柿	xīhóngshì (PRC)
汽水	qìshuǐ	鸡蛋	jīdàn		
牛奶	niúnǎi	番茄	fānqié (TW)		

Additional useful vocabulary

牌价	páijià	N	list price (PRC)
斤	jīn	N	unit of weight; ½ kilogram
束	shù	M	a bunch of
罐	guàn	N	a can (of soda, beer, etc.)
只	zhī	M	for birds, some animals, one of a pair of things
枝	zhī	M	for long, thin objects (pens, cigarettes, etc.) and for flowers with stems intact
农民	nóngmín	N	farmer
稍微	shāowēi	Adv	slightly

You are planning to cook a meal tonight and so you need to go shopping. What kinds of food and drink would you expect to find at a public market? List five to eight items.

_____

_____

_____

_____

_____

_____

_____

_____

_____

 **Listening for the Gist**

Who are the speakers in this conversation?

- ❑ Two customers.
- ❑ A customer and a farmer.
- ❑ Two farmers.
- ❑ A reporter and a farmer.

Which sections of this recording are repeated? (circle one)

One and two.   Two and three.   One and three.

🔍 Listening for Details

Fill in the prices and the appropriate measure word for each item mentioned. Be careful—not all the items listed below are in the report.

海虾 ＿＿＿元／＿＿＿＿　　　鸡腿 ＿＿＿元／＿＿＿

牛肉 ＿＿＿元／＿＿＿＿　　　白菜 ＿＿＿元／＿＿＿

草鱼 ＿＿＿元／＿＿＿＿　　　玫瑰花＿＿＿元／＿＿＿

啤酒 ＿＿＿元／＿＿＿＿　　　菊花 ＿＿＿元／＿＿＿

可乐 ＿＿＿元／＿＿＿＿　　　汽水 ＿＿＿元／＿＿＿

番茄 ＿＿＿元／＿＿＿＿　　　鸡蛋 ＿＿＿元／＿＿＿

米 ＿＿＿元／＿＿＿＿　　　牛奶 ＿＿＿元／＿＿＿

生菜 ＿＿＿元／＿＿＿＿

What is the man being interviewed selling today?

	✓		✓
牛肉		鱼	
虾		鸡蛋	
番茄		生菜	
汽水		鸡	
啤酒			

他卖的东西比以前 ...

	✓
稍微便宜了。	
便宜多了。	
稍微贵了。	
贵多了。	
一样。	
他沒说。	

那是因为 ...

	✓
沒有人买他的东西。	
他沒有钱。	
几个月以前下大雨了。	
几个月都没有下雨。	

 **Working with the Language**

Some measure words function the same way in Chinese as in English. For example, in this recording you heard that in Chinese a can of soda is _____. Write the appropriate Chinese characters for the following. A list of possible measure words is given to get you started.

块　本　枝　双　碗　片　罐　条　瓶　束　张　杯　位　件

a cup of tea

_____

a bottle of wine

_____

a slice of bread （面包 miànbāo）

_____

a bowl of rice

_____

a pair of chopsticks （筷子 kuàizi）

_____

a bunch of flowers

_____

a chunk of meat

_____

a can of beer

_____

Review some of the other measure words you have learned by writing the appropriate mw for each of these nouns.

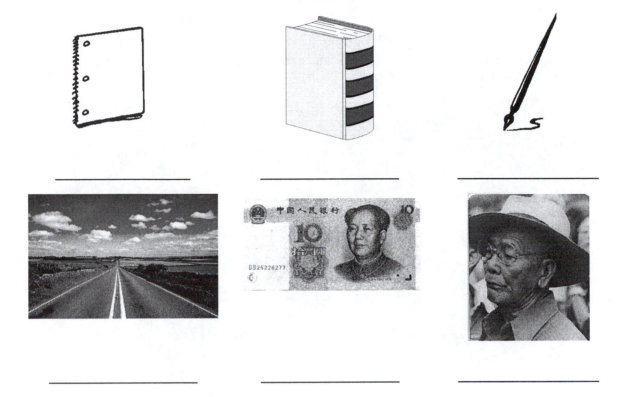

_____   _____   _____

_____   _____   _____

✳ ✳ ✳

At the end of the interview the reporter says to the farmer: 啊，是这样吗? How would you translate this question? Does it require an answer? Why or why not?

_____

_____

Think of two other situations when it might be appropriate to say this. Create two short dialogues in which this would be the final comment a person would say.

1. 甲： _____

_____

_____

乙：啊，是这样吗?

2. 甲： _____

_____

_____

乙：啊，是这样吗?

⇘ **Follow-up Activities**

大家来说 Role-playing (oral)

Here are some photos taken that day at the public market. With a partner talk about each picture, making sure you describe what is being sold and how it is displayed.

 大家来写 **Role-playing (written)**

Now imagine that you overhear a conversation between one of the farmers and a customer. The customer has a number of items s/he wants to buy but first wants to know the price, wants to know if the food is fresh (xīnxiān 新鲜), and also needs some help knowing how much to buy. Of course it's always a good idea to bargain a little, too. Write down (in pīnyīn or characters) what this dialogue might be like.

_____

_____

_____

_____

_____

_____

_____

Lesson 25 (CD2.2) 第二十五课
Getting Together 約朋友出去玩

 **Preparation**

Useful vocabulary

灯笼	dēnglǒng	N	lantern
挂	guà	V	to hang
小时	xiǎoshí	N	an hour (cf. 钟头)
不过	búguò	Conj	but, however (cf. 可是)
门口	ménkǒu	N	entrance

Do you like to plan getting together with friends in advance or do you like to do things spontaneously? Think about the last time you initiated getting together to do something with someone and jot down whether you planned it for a long time, whether you ended up doing what you originally had in mind, and what you might want to do with that person the next time you get together. Do you think your attitude toward doing things with friends would be different if you were a student living in China? In what ways?

Listening for the Gist

Who made the phone call (circle one)

     Haning   Yingnan

Who seems to be busier?

     Haning   Yingnan

Haning and Yingnan planned to go …

- ❑ to the zoo.
- ❑ to the movies.
- ❑ rollerskating.
- ❑ out to eat.
- ❑ to the museum.

Listening for Details

Check all the times that were mentioned.

	✓		✓
today		Saturday at noon	
this afternoon at 1:00		Saturday afternoon	
this evening		Sunday morning	
Saturday morning		Sunday at noon	
Sunday afternoon		Saturday 1:00 p.m	
Sunday 1:00 p.m.		tomorrow	

Yingnan was free to go on …

- ❑ Saturday morning.
- ❑ Saturday evening.
- ❑ Sunday afternoon.
- ❑ Saturday at noon.

Haning and Yingnan planned to meet …

- ❑ at the gate of the Beijing zoo.
- ❑ at the entrance to the New China Bookstore.
- ❑ near Mao's mausoleum on Tian'anmen Square.
- ❑ at the Dahua Theater.

Who says 不见不散?

     Haning   Yingnan

What is the best translation for this comment?

	✓
If I don't see you I won't leave.	
Don't leave before you see me.	
I won't see you until I'm done.	

166

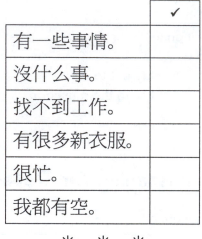 **Working with the Language**

What would be an appropriate response to the question 有沒有什么事? (check all that apply)

	✓
有一些事情。	
沒什么事。	
找不到工作。	
有很多新衣服。	
很忙。	
我都有空。	

✱   ✱   ✱

Fill in the Chinese characters and pīnyīn for "Raise the Red Lantern."

汉字	pīnyīn
_____ _____灯笼_____高挂	dàhóng_____ _____gāo_____guà

 **Follow-up Activities**

大家来说 **Role-playing (oral)**

What do you like to do on the weekends? With a partner take turns inviting each other to join you in this activity (in Chinese). Be sure to find out if the person likes this activity, when you both are free, and where you will meet.

大家来写 **Role-playing (written)**

Here is a weekly calendar. Make a note about the activity that Haning and Yingnan have planned in the "Things to do this week" section. Include all pertinent information in Chinese, i.e., date, time, meeting place, activity, etc. In addition, make appointments (in Chinese) with three different classmates and record them on the proper days at the proper time.

Planner

星期一	
8:00	
9:00	
10:00	
11:00	
12:00	
1:00	
2:00	
3:00	
4:00	
5:00	

星期 二	
8:00	
9:00	
10:00	
11:00	
12:00	
1:00	
2:00	
3:00	
4:00	
5:00	

Things to do this week

星期三	
8:00	
9:00	
10:00	
11:00	
12:00	
1:00	
2:00	
3:00	
4:00	
5:00	

星期四	
8:00	
9:00	
10:00	
11:00	
12:00	
1:00	
2:00	
3:00	
4:00	
5:00	

Notes

星期五	
8:00	
9:00	
10:00	
11:00	
12:00	
1:00	
2:00	
3:00	
4:00	
5:00	

星期六	
8:00	
9:00	
10:00	
11:00	
12:00	
1:00	
2:00	
3:00	
4:00	
5:00	

Lesson 26 (CD2.3) 第二十六课
Getting Lost 迷路

 **Preparation**

Useful vocabulary

沿	yán	V	to follow, to go along
侧	cè	N	side
步行	bùxíng	V	to go on foot
动物园	dòngwùyuán	N	zoo
正	zhèng	Adv	precisely, exactly
对	duì	Adj	facing, opposite
米	mǐ	N	meter
标志	biāozhì	N	sign, mark
石头	shítou	N, Adj	stone
狮子	shīzi	N	lion (石狮子)
迷	mí	V	to lose one's bearings, to become confused (迷路)

When you ask someone for directions, do you visualize in your mind where you need to go? As an experiment, ask the person next to you for directions to the library. As they give you directions, sketch out a map below. Switch roles when finished.

Listening for the Gist

The conversation is between …

	✓
two friends.	
two strangers.	
a passenger and a bus driver.	
a mother and a daughter.	

The woman is asking directions to …

	✓
the zoo.	
a bus stop.	
a bookstore.	
a market.	

Check all the places you heard mentioned in this conversation.

	✓
the market	
Beijing Xinhua Bookstore	
Nanhua Cafeteria	
#10 bus stop	
the zoo	
Beijing library	
Guangming Theater	

Check the different modes of transportation you heard mentioned.

	✓
bus	
car	
walking	
taxi	

Listening for Details

In order to arrive at her destination, Yingnan needs to follow the directions in the proper sequence. Number the instructions below in their proper order, according to the conversation.

	#
Get off the bus at the zoo.	
Get on the #10 bus.	
Walk straight ahead (left of the Beijing Library) for about five minutes.	
Walk straight ahead (on the right side of the zoo) for 100 meters.	
Look for the stone lions.	

Working with the Language

The person giving directions uses the construction verb + 著 zhe twice in her explanation. Here are the two passages in which these comments occur. Go back and listen to her directions and fill in the blanks accordingly. Some additional blank spaces have been left for you to fill in, too.

1. 你_____著这个北京图书馆，它的_____侧，向前走，…然后你就会看到一个_____站。

2. 下车以后你_____这个动物园大门口，它的_____侧，再往前走一百米_____了。

Choose the letter of the word from column B that is a synonym or or definition for the word in column B.

Column A	Column B
____ 步行	a. 不远
____ 明白	b. 不多
____ 向	c. 很
____ 非常	d. 懂
____ 很近	e. 往
	f. 走路

Follow-up Activities

大家来说 Role-playing (oral)

On the map, write in the Chinese characters for the street names. Then draw in the location of the bus station, the hotel, the hospital, and the market, using the symbols below the map. With a partner take turns asking where each place is located, starting at the arrow in the bottom right corner of the map.

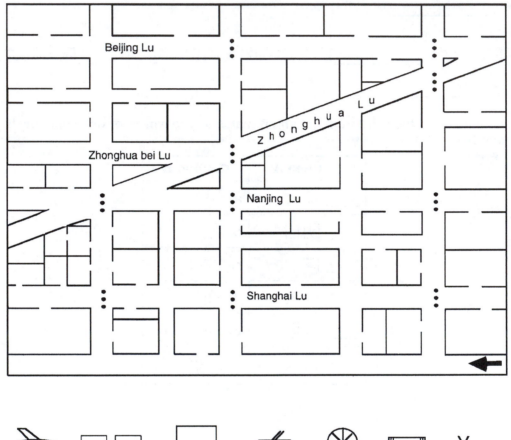

Beijing Lu

Zhonghua Lu

Zhonghua bei Lu

Nanjing Lu

Shanghai Lu

 airport   train station   bus station   restaurant   cinema   theatre   bank

hotel   post office   police station   hospital   market   gas station

大家来写 **Role-playing (written)**

Here are two pictures of the West Entrance at Beijing University. In Chinese list five interesting features you notice.

_____

_____

_____

_____

_____

_____

_____

_____

_____

_____

_____

_____

_____

_____

_____

Lesson 27 (CD2.4) 第二十七课
Arriving Late 迟到

 **Preparation**

Useful Vocabulary

回	huí	MW for 事	
		V	to return, go back
搞	gǎo	V	(colloq.) to do, to work, to manage, etc.
反	fǎn	Adj	opposite
出发	chūfā	V	to set out
头发	tóufa (tóufǎ)	N	hair
理发店	lǐfādiàn , lǐfǎdiàn	N	hair salon (cf. 美容院 měiróngyuàn: beauty parlor)
剪	jiǎn	V	to cut
排队	páiduì	V	to stand in line
陪	péi	V	to accompany

Draw a line connecting each Chinese expression to its English equivalent.

怎么回事(儿)	I'm sorry.
怎么搞的	Not bad!
对不起	Is anything the matter?
沒关系	Don't mention it; you're welcome.
真不错	What happened?

You made plans to meet a friend at a specific time, but you arrived late. What conversation might occur between you and your friend once you arrive? List five things that might be said.

_____

_____

_____

_____

_____

_____

_____

_____

Listening for the Gist

Of the following topics, indicate which ones you heard mentioned in the dialogue:

	✓
Why Yingnan arrived later.	
The time when Yingnan arrived.	
Making an apology.	
The location where they met.	
The reason they got together.	
The weather.	
Wearing new clothes.	
Getting a haircut.	
Riding the bus.	
Watching a movie.	

🔍 Listening for Details

Please complete the following sentences according to what you heard in the dialogue. Put a check by the correct answer.

Yingnan was late because she …

	✓
lost track of time.	
missed the bus.	
took the wrong bus.	
was getting a haircut.	

Yingnan and Haning plan to …

	✓
go shopping.	
have lunch together.	
go see a movie.	
get their hair cut.	

They finally left together at …

	✓
12:00.	
2:00.	
2:35.	
12:35.	
5:35.	

Who got a haircut?

        Yingnan   Haning   Yingnan and Haning

Her/their haircut(s) cost …

	✓
$10.00.	
$18.00.	
$8.00.	
$15.00.	

Indicate who said the following lines by filling in the number under each name.

Yingnan said:	Haning said:

1. "我来晚了。"

2. "我那个车子坐错了。"

3. "你今天的裙子很漂亮。"

4. "是新买的吗？"

5. "你的头发很漂亮。"

7. "人好多，都在排队。"

8. "我陪你去。"

9. "那我们快点儿走吧。"

10. "来不及了吧。"

(***Note:** Really she should have said "其实还不算太贵。")

* * *

英南上了几路公共汽车？

- ❑ 四路车
- ❑ 十路车
- ❑ 四十路车
- ❑ 十四路车

Working with the Language

Provide subjects for these verb phrases based on what you heard in the dialogue. You can write in either pīnyīn or Chinese characters.

1. _____ 走错了

2. _____ 看完了

3. _____ 反了

4. _____ 走回来了

5. _____ 新买的

6. _____ 昨天剪的

7. _____ 挺有名的

＊　＊　＊

Toward the beginning of this conversation Yingnan says 结果问了一个人． 结果 means "as a result, it ended up that." Complete the following sentences using 结果.

Example:

我本来要坐十九路车，结果

↳我本来要坐十九路车，结果坐了十路车，坐错了。

1. 哈宁昨天说她不要剪头发，结果 ...

_____

2. 英南告诉她男朋友她很喜欢这条裙子，结果 ...

_____

3. 哈宁跟英南 12:50 才到了电影院，结果 ...

_____

⬎ Follow-up Activities

大家来说 Role-playing (oral)

Later that day Haning got her hair cut, did some shopping, and ran a few other errands. A friend of hers stopped by to visit in the evening. Enact their conversation as they talked about what they each had done recently. Be sure to use at least the following vocabulary items:

随便　结果　其实　头发　排队　time word 才 verb　怎么搞的　剪　回来　来不及

大家来写 Role-playing (reading)

While Haning was waiting to get her hair cut, she read about a new book club that is being organized in Hong Kong and decided to fill out an application form. How would you fill out this form? Below are some hints to help you out.

請塗膠水並封口

好文書會入會申請表格

中文姓名 _____ 性別 _____

英文姓名 _____

職業 _____ 教育程度 _____

年齡（請在□加√） □ 24 歲以下 　　□ 25 歲 -30 歲
□ 31 歲 -40 歲 　　□ 41 歲 -50 歲 　　□ 50 歲以上

地址 _____

_____

電話 _____ 圖文傳真 _____

E-MAIL : _____

請塗膠水並封口

閱 讀 興 趣

（請在□加√，最高限選 5 類，如全部均有興趣只需填第 1 類）

01 □ 全部　　　　02 □ 哲學　　　03 □ 社會科學、政治
04 □ 經濟　　　　05 □ 軍事　　　06 □ 法律
07 □ 文化、教育　　08 □ 藝術　　09 □ 語言、文字
1A □ 中國文學　　1B □ 外國文學　11 □ 歷史、文化、考古
12 □ 地理　　　　13 □ 自然科學　1C □ 中醫
1D □ 西醫　　　　15 □ 工程技術　16 □ 農林、畜牧、漁
17 □ 綜合參考(年鑑百科全書)　　　18 □ 體育、健身、保健
19 □ 生活、娛樂 20 □ 旅遊　　　21 □ 兒童讀物
22 □ 連環圖　　　57 □ 字典辭典　59 □ 線裝書
60 □ 畫冊圖書　　62 □ 紅學研究　63 □ 魯迅研究

申 請 人 簽 署

□ 本人願意加入好文書會、享用書會提供給會員的專有服務，
　並付上劃線支票／銀行本票港幣／美元／加元／英鎊／澳
　元_____ 元，繳付好文書會年費。

簽署： X 　　　　　　　　日期：

請塗膠水並封口

Helpful vocabulary

性別	xìngbié	N	sex
職業（职业）	zhíyè	N	occupation
教育程度	jiàoyùchéngdù	N	level of education
以下/以上		Suf	below; under/ above; over
限	xiàn	V	to set a limit, to restrict
類（类）	lèi	N	categories
填	tián	V	to fill out
			(e.g., 填表 tiánbiǎo: to fill out a form)
服務（服务）	fúwù	N	service
支票	zhīpiào	N	check

Answer the following questions in English based on this form.

1. Where should you write your address and fax number?

_____

_____

2. In the second section, under what circumstances should you check the box marked 01?

_____

_____

3. What is the most number of categories you are advised to check?

_____

_____

4. If you were interested in dictionaries, which box would you check? _____

How about Chinese medicine? _____

Economics? _____   Linguistics? _____

Natural science? _____   Travel? _____

Archaeology? _____

5. What different types of currency are mentioned in the third section of the form?

_____

_____

6. If you check the box in the third section, what do you need to circle and what do you need to fill in?

_____

_____

7. If you sign, date, and mail in this form, what have you agreed to ?

_____

_____

Lesson 28 (CD2.5)　第二十八课
Apartment Hunting　找房子

 **Preparation**

Useful vocabulary

拜托	bàituō	V	trouble someone with, request someone to do something
带	dài	V	to have something attached, to take, to carry
盥洗室	guànxǐshì	N	washroom
浴缸	yùgāng	N	bath tub
商量	shāngliang	V	discuss, talk over

Idiomatic phrases

那就算了　　"Then forget it."　"Then it's okay."

这样吧　　"How about this?"　"Let's do it this way."

When apartment hunting, what factors do you take into consideration? What features do you look for? List five of your concerns below.

_____

_____

_____

_____

_____

_____

_____

Listening for the Gist

Which of the following topics did Yingnan and Haning mention in this conversation?

	✓
The favor Yingnan requests.	
Where she wants to find an apartment.	
Where she is currently living.	
The amount she can afford to pay for rent.	
Why she plans to move.	
Whether she wants an apartment with a private kitchen.	
Whether she wants an apartment with a private bathroom.	
Whether she wants an apartment with a bathtub.	
When she plans to move.	
The number of bedrooms she wants.	

Does Haning seem able to help Yingnan find an apartment? How can you tell?

_____

_____

 # Listening for Details

Circle whether the statement is true (是) or false (非):

Yingnan wants a two-bedroom apartment.   是   非

Yingnan thinks 250 RMB is too much to pay for rent.   是   非

Yingnan thinks it would be best to have an apartment with a kitchen.   是   非

Yingnan does not really need a bathtub in the apartment.   是   非

Haning thinks Yingnan could get a one bedroom apartment for 250 RMB.   是   非

How does Haning offer to help Yingnan find an apartment?

	✓
Take her to see an apartment.	
Introduce her to someone she knows who has a vacant apartment.	
Introduce her to someone she knows whose job is apartment rentals.	

When are they planning to leave?

	✓
Right now.	
After lunch.	
After they call Haning's friend.	
After they call about the apartment.	

Working with the Language

In this conversation Yingnan says: 我有一件事情要拜托你. How would you translate this sentence?

_____

In Chinese there are many polite ways to ask for someone's assistance or to get their attention. 请问 and 对不起 ("excuse me," "pardon me") are most common and least formal and are often followed by a question of substance (e.g., 请问，现在几点钟？). 拜托 is more limited in usage; it is used when someone is asking someone to do a favor. 劳驾 láojià, an expression used by northern Chinese speakers, is similar to 拜托.

Sometimes 麻烦 is used as a polite way of asking someone to do something, i.e., "may I trouble you to …" But it has many other meanings.

麻烦 máfan	V	to trouble, to disturb (cf. 打扰 dǎrǎo: to disturb, (more formal than 麻烦)
	Adj	troublesome, bothersome
	N	trouble, annoyance

Examples. See if you can translate these sentences into English.

1. 英南觉得找房子真麻烦。

_____

2. 她不愿意麻烦哈宁，可是她沒有别的办法。

_____

3. 她说我以后不会给你很多麻烦。

Now fill in the blanks using one of the following terms. In some cases there is more than one correct answer.

拜托　　麻烦　　请问　　对不起

1. 我想_____你一件事。

2. 哈宁非常愿意帮英南的忙，她觉得一点也不_____。

3. _____，你有时间陪我找房子吗？

4. 如果不太_____，你可不可以送我回家？

5. 请你帮我一个忙。_____ _____。

6. _____，你可不可以带我去看一个房子。

7. _____ 你把那张地图给我。

8. 住在没有厨房的公寓太_____。

9. _____，这个公寓的盥洗室带不带浴缸？

10. 哈宁的朋友今天有一点不舒服，你最好别_____她。

✳　✳　✳

Cross out the one word of this group that is not a near synonym.

前后	qiánhòu
左右	zuǒyòu
早晚	zǎowǎn
差不多	chàbuduō
上下	shàngxià

Follow-up Activities

The next day Yingnan went to look at two apartments. Fill in the information to complete these advertisements based on the floor plans described. Based on what Yingnan said in her conversation with Haning, which apartment would she probably choose?

A _____   B _____

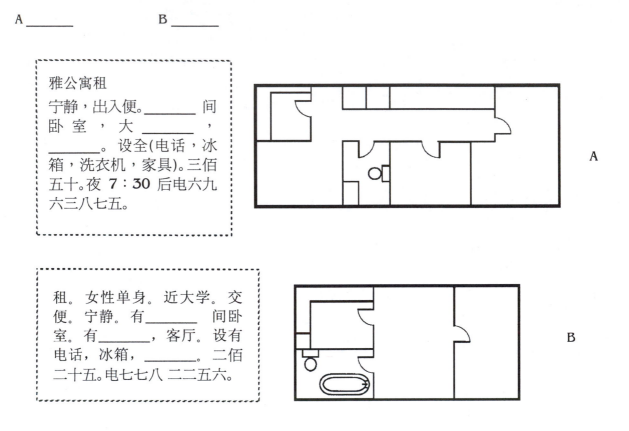

雅公寓租
宁静，出入便。_____ 间
卧室，大 _____，
_____。设全(电话，冰
箱，洗衣机，家具)。三佰
五十。夜 7：30 后电六九
六三八七五。

租。女性单身。近大学。交
便。宁静。有_____ 间卧
室。有_____，客厅。设有
电话，冰箱，_____。二佰
二十五。电七七八 二二五六。

大家来说 Role-playing (oral)

Here's a photo of another apartment building that Yingnan looked at. With a partner imagine that you and she were looking at an apartment in this building and that you also thought of a list of questions to ask the landlord and some of the other tenants who live there.

Lesson 29 (CD2.6) 第二十八课
Learning to Cook Chinese Food
学做中国菜

 **Preparation**

Useful vocabulary

普通	pǔtōng	Adj	common, ordinary
家常菜	jiāchángcài	N	family-style dish, home cooking
打散	dǎsǎn	V	to break up, to beat
搁	gē	V	to place, to add (cf. 放)
创造	chuàngzào	V	to invent, to create
炖	dùn	V	to marinate
尝(一尝)	chángyìcháng	V	to taste
首先	shǒuxiān	Adv	first (in a series of things)
		Conj	in the first place, first of all
新鲜	xīnxiān	Adj	fresh
菊花	júhuā	N	chrysanthemum
干	gān	Adj	dry
泡(开)	pào(kāi)	V	to soak, to steep (e.g., 泡茶)

 **Listening for the Gist**

How many dishes did the cook prepare?

_____

Check which ingredients were mentioned.

- ❑ eggs
- ❑ salt
- ❑ tomatoes
- ❑ onions
- ❑ garlic
- ❑ sugar
- ❑ ginger
- ❑ chicken
- ❑ shrimp

❑ beef   ❑ fish   ❑ MSG
❑ wine   ❑ cola   ❑ vinegar
❑ oil   ❑ soy sauce

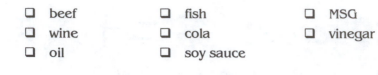

Listening for Details

In Chinese give the name of each dish and list at least three ingredients that are in it.

_____

_____

_____

Which dish is an authentic Cantonese recipe? _____

Which dish was invented by the cook being interviewed? _____

Which dish is a family-style dish? _____

Give the proper order for the steps for steaming a fish, based on the explanation given by this cook.

做法	#
把鱼洗一洗	
几分钟就可以，不要蒸得太老	
把鱼放进锅里蒸	
搁点盐，糖跟酱油	
放上一点菊花	

If you are unable to find fresh chrysanthemum flowers, what can be substituted and how should they be prepared?

_____

Working with the Language

Write the letter from column B of the definition or synonym of each word in Column A.

Column A	Column B
_____ 普通	a. 想出新方法
_____ 简单	b. 吃一口

Column A	Column B
_____ 首先	c. 第一
_____ 搁	d. 调味儿
_____ 别	e. 可以
_____ 创造	f. 放
_____ 行	g. 平常的；一般的
_____ 尝一尝	h. 不要
	i. 容易

* * *

千万不要　千万别 "By all means don't"

The chef uses the expression 千万不要 twice in this interview. Write down what she says exactly in Chinese:

千万不要

_____

千万不要

_____

Complete the dialogues with a sentence using 千万不要 (or 千万别) that makes sense based on the information given in the first speaker's comment sentence.

Example:

甲：我已经觉得很累了。

乙：那你千万不要再跑了。

1.　甲：我母亲昨天给我的钱快用完了。

　　乙：_____

2.　甲：这个菜本来很咸。(xián: salty)

　　乙：_____

3. 甲：过年的时候，我父母要请几位客人吃饭。

   乙：＿＿＿＿＿＿＿＿＿＿＿＿＿＿＿＿＿＿＿＿＿＿＿＿＿

4. 甲：那条鱼好像不太新鲜了。

   乙：＿＿＿＿＿＿＿＿＿＿＿＿＿＿＿＿＿＿＿＿＿＿＿＿＿

5. 甲：炒饭的做法很简单，可是我做得沒有你做得好。

   乙：＿＿＿＿＿＿＿＿＿＿＿＿＿＿＿＿＿＿＿＿＿＿＿＿＿

➘ Follow-up Activities

大家来说 Role-playing (oral)

With a partner take turns acting out and explaining in Chinese how to make at least one of the dishes described in this interview. Be sure to mention what ingredients are needed （材料) and how the dish should be prepared (做法).

大家来写 Role-playing (written)

Interview someone you know who cooks Chinese food. Find out what his or her favorite dish to prepare (拿手菜 náshǒucài) is and write down the recipe in Chinese.

Name of the dish: ＿＿＿＿＿＿＿＿＿＿＿＿＿＿＿＿＿＿＿＿＿＿＿

Name of the chef: ＿＿＿＿＿＿＿＿＿＿＿＿＿＿＿＿＿＿＿＿＿＿

材料：

＿＿＿＿＿＿＿＿＿＿＿＿＿＿＿＿＿＿＿＿＿＿＿＿＿＿＿＿＿＿＿＿＿

＿＿＿＿＿＿＿＿＿＿＿＿＿＿＿＿＿＿＿＿＿＿＿＿＿＿＿＿＿＿＿＿＿

＿＿＿＿＿＿＿＿＿＿＿＿＿＿＿＿＿＿＿＿＿＿＿＿＿＿＿＿＿＿＿＿＿

＿＿＿＿＿＿＿＿＿＿＿＿＿＿＿＿＿＿＿＿＿＿＿＿＿＿＿＿＿＿＿＿＿

＿＿＿＿＿＿＿＿＿＿＿＿＿＿＿＿＿＿＿＿＿＿＿＿＿＿＿＿＿＿＿＿＿

做法：

_____

_____

_____

_____

_____

Lesson 30 (CD2.7) 第三十课
Medical Examination 身体检查

 **Preparation**

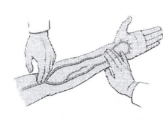

_____

_____

_____

| 脉搏 | màibó | 舌头 | shétou | 脖子 | bózi | 脑袋疼 | nǎodài téng (头疼) |
| 疲劳 | píláo | 大夫 | dàifu | 体温 | tǐwēn | | |

Useful vocabulary

伸	shēn	V	to stretch out, to stick out (伸出来)
正常	zhèngcháng	Adj	normal
胃口	wèikǒu	N	appetite
赶	gǎn	V	to rush to finish, to rush to work on
论文	lùnwén	N	thesis, dissertation, research paper or article
睡眠	shuìmián	N	sleep
初期	chūqī	N	elementary, first stage
冲剂	chōngjì	N	medicine that needs to be mixed with water
袋	dài	N	packet
有效	yǒuxiào	V O	efficacious, effective, gets results (cf. 有用，有效果 yǒu xiàoguǒ)

When you are ill, do you usually go to see a doctor? If so, what questions does the doctor ask you? If not, what kind of home remedies do you use? Do you make changes in your diet or other daily habits?

194

Write the letter from Column B of the definition or synonym of each word in Column A:

Column A	Column B
____ 老 （老是）	a. 一个星期
____ 理解 lǐjiě	b. 非常累
____ 脑袋	c. 气力小
____ 熬夜 āoyè	d. 医生
____ 弱 ruò	e. 经常
____ 疲劳	f. 懂
____ 一周	g. 深夜不睡觉
____ 大夫	h. 头

 **Listening for the Gist**

Check all the topics mentioned in this conversation.

	✓
Where she doesn't feel well.	
Whether she has a fever.	
Whether she has been coughing.	
Whether she is now taking any medicine.	
What she normally eats.	
What she normally drinks.	
If she sleeps well.	
If she gets regular exercise.	
What her occupation is.	

How would you describe this doctor's attitude toward his patient? Do you think the patient will follow his advice? Why or why not?

_____

_____

Listening for Details

Check all that apply.

The patient was going to the doctor because she …

- ❑ had an accident.
- ❑ has a headache.
- ❑ is tired.
- ❑ drinks too much coffee.
- ❑ has gastro-intestinal pains.

She was suffering from pain in …

- ❑ her shoulder.
- ❑ her knee.
- ❑ the left side of her head.
- ❑ her eyes.

She is experiencing the most discomfort …

- ❑ in the morning.
- ❑ in the afternoon.
- ❑ after meals.
- ❑ in the evening.

According to the doctor, she is ill because she …

- ❑ is not sleeping enough.
- ❑ needs more fiber in her diet.
- ❑ is drinking too much coffee.
- ❑ has too much stress in her life.

After identifying the patient's symptoms, the doctor diagnosed her as having …

- ❑ allergies.
- ❑ a stomach ache.
- ❑ a cold.
- ❑ insomnia.

The doctor advised her to …

- ❑ drink less coffee.
- ❑ rest more.
- ❑ take digestive aids.
- ❑ sleep more.
- ❑ take aspirin.

The patient should take the medicine the doctor prescribed …

- ❑ once daily.
- ❑ twice daily.
- ❑ as needed.
- ❑ after meals.
- ❑ three times daily.

How long should the patient wait to see if there is an improvement?

- ❑ A few days.
- ❑ One week.
- ❑ Ten days.
- ❑ Two weeks.

 **Working with the Language**

多/少

In this conversation the doctor recommends that the patient do what more and what less? In both cases he uses the construction subject 多/少 + verb.

_____

_____

Complete the following sentences using 多 or 少, depending on the context. Add whatever additional information is necessary to make the sentence complete.

Example:

我今天非常饿，要_____一碗饭。

↳ 我今天非常饿，要多吃一碗饭。

1. 外边很冷，你应该_____一点衣服。

2. 每天吃肉对身体不好。你应该_____一点。

3. 如果你体温不正常的话，要_____。

4. 这本书只要八块钱。你_____给了_____块。

5.赶论文的时候要_____ 喝_____。

＊　＊　＊

多 and 少 are also used in other ways. See if you can translate these sentences into English and explain the function of each occurrence of 多 and 少.

1. 她以前病得很厉害，现在看起来好多了。

_____

_____

2. 本来有十六个学生要来吃饭，现在少了两个。

_____

_____

3. 有的人说得多，做得少。

_____

_____

4. 今天饭做少了，恐怕不够吃。

_____

_____

5. 我们是多年的老朋友了，我一定要请他吃饭。

_____

_____

6. 他们家什么都有，什么东西都不少。

_____

_____

7. 这个地方的天气太糟糕，我不能在这儿长住。

_____

_____

8. 你少来这一套。(yītào: phony promise, insincere gesture)

_____

_____

9. 你这个字多写了一笔。

_____

_____

10. 请你多多指教。(zhǐjiào: to instruct, polite expression for asking someone's criticisms)

_____

_____

＊　＊　＊

左右

When the doctor asks the patient about her temperature, what does she say (in Chinese)?

_____

How would you translate her statement?

_____

Here are some other ways of expressing approximation. In some cases these terms can be used synonymously.

1. 左右   zuǒyòu   around, more or less (used after numbers or after number + measure word)

2. 前后   qiánhòu   around, more or less; altogether

3. 上下   shàngxià   around, more or less

4. 差不多   chàbuduō   almost, nearly

5. 几乎   jīhū   almost

6. 差一点兒   chà(yi)diǎn(r)   almost

7. number + 来 (used after 十，百，千，万) = approximately (cf. number+多)

8. 一般   yìbān   most, in general

9. 大多数   dàduōshù   the great majority

Fill in the blanks with the number(s) of the expression(s) from the list above that indicate(s) an approximation in each sentence. In some cases you will need to give more than one answer. Then translate the completed sentence.

1. 那个病人等了_____两个小时。(2 choices)

_____

2. 同时 (at the same time) 大概有十_____个人也在那儿等。

_____

3. 虽然这个医院有_____三百个病房,可是_____的病人不住院。
(1 choice; 2 choices)

_____

4. _____人都等到非常不舒服的时候，才找医生看病。(2 choices)

_____

5. 王大夫星期五非常忙， 她_____忘了吃饭。(2 choices)

_____

6. 那种药相当贵，二十片要十八块钱_____。

⇘ **Follow-up Activities**

🖎 大家来写 **Role-playing (written)**

Imagine that you are the doctor in this case. Take notes about this patient's condition in your medical journal. Make sure to include her symptoms, your diagnosis, what medication you prescribed, what advice you gave her, etc. Write in Chinese.

👥 大家来说 **Role-playing (oral)**

A few weeks later this patient was still not feeling well, so she went to see the doctor again. With a partner, act out this conversation. Make sure you at least use the following vocabulary items: 有效，左右，疲劳，正常，subject 多/少+verb, 疼得... (or 痛得...)，熬夜，睡眠，弱，休息。

Lesson 31 (CD2.8) 第三十一课
Traffic Accident 车祸

 **Preparation**

Useful vocabulary

司机	sījī	N	driver
慌	huāng	Adj	to be anxious, upset, scared
冲	chōng	V	to collide, to crash
闪(开)	shǎn(kaī)	V	to avoid, to get out of the way
撞	zhuàng	V	to run into, to strike
受伤	shòushāng	V O	to receive an injury, to be injured
玻璃	bōlí	N	glass
失去知觉	shīqùzhījué	V O	to lose consciousness
流血	liúxuè, liúxuě	V O	to bleed (also pronounced xiě)
系	jì	V	to fasten, to tie
安全带	ānquándài	N	seat belt
幸亏	xìngkuī	Adv	fortunately
保险	bǎoxiǎn	N	insurance
		V	to insure
凹(进去)	wā, āo	Adj	sunken, dented, concave (cf. 凸 tū: protruding)
陷(进去)	xiàn	Adj	caved in, sunken
碎	suì	V	to be smashed
突然	tūrán	Adv	suddenly
拖	tuō	V	to haul away
幺	yāo	Nu	一, used orally for the numeral one

Have you ever been in a car accident? Were the police involved? If so, how did they handle the situation? If you were a police officer in charge of investigating a traffic accident, what would you do when you first arrived on the scene?

_____

_____

_____

_____

_____

_____

_____

_____

Circle the number of cars that were involved in the accident.

What kinds of questions did the policemen ask?

	✓
If her seatbelt was fastened.	
If she used her blinker.	
If she lost consciousness.	
What happened.	
If she was hurt.	
If she had the license plate number of the other car.	
If anyone else was hurt.	

	✓
If she had been drinking.	
If she is the owner of the car.	
Personal information (name, where she lives, works, etc.).	
If she needs to go to the hospital.	

Toward the end of the conversation, what information did the woman offer? (check all that apply)

	✓
Her telephone number.	
The number on her driver's license.	
The number of her license plate.	
The license plate number of the other car.	
The name of her insurance company.	

Listening for Details

Check the appropriate box based on the information in this conversation.

	Wang Hong's car	The red car
On Beijing Rd.		
On Zhongshan Rd.		
Stopped at the red light.		
Ran through the red light.		
Restarted when the light turned green.		
Turned right on Beijing Rd.		
Turned left on Zhongshan Rd.		
Was hit from the left.		
Was hit from the right.		

Indicate the location of vehicle(s) when accident occurred and the direction of travel:

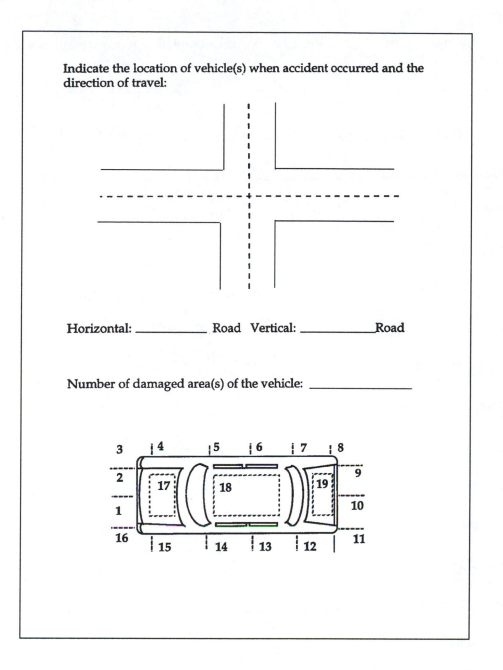

Horizontal: _____ Road   Vertical: _____ Road

Number of damaged area(s) of the vehicle: _____

Based on the information given in the conversation, complete the investigator's traffic accident report.

INVESTIGATOR'S TRAFFIC ACCIDENT REPORT

Date of Accident: _____ Time: _____

City: _____ Investigator's Name: _____

Investigated at Scene: Y   N

Number Killed: _____ Number Injured: _____

Location: _____ Road(s)

Total Vehicle(s) Involved: _____

Driver's Name: _____   Sex: M   F

Office (dānwèi): _____ Phone: _____

Driver's Lic. No.: _____ Date of Birth: _____

Violation(s):   Y   N   (if yes) _____

Lic. Plate No.: _____ Body Type: _____

Insurance Policy #: _____

Vehicle Towed: Y   N

Wang Hong had to fill out an insurance form giving the details of the accident. As you can imagine, she was still somewhat shaken up by the experience and so she left out quite a few words. Can you help her complete the report? Use Chinese characters.

我把车_____在_____路的_____灯前。大概过了_____分钟，换成了_____灯，我就_____拐，拐进_____路。突然，一辆_____色的车从我的_____边直冲过来。我来_____及闪开，就被它撞了。

Working with the Language

Here are some excerpts from this conversation. First indicate who the speaker of each line is (male or female) and then indicate what the conversational function of the line is (choose the number of the functions listed below). For example, is the speaker trying to get information, offer advice, ask for clarification, etc.?

Conversational Functions

1. advising/suggesting
2. asking for information
3. assuming
4. giving an order
5. reaching a conclusion
6. denying
7. complying with a request
8. answering a question/giving information
9. repeating
10. requesting clarification
11. asking for advice

男 女　　走开!走开!车祸有什么好看呢？都走开!　　____

男 女　　你是这辆车的司机吗？　　____

男 女　　对，我就开这辆车。　　____

男 女　　你的姓名？　　____

男 女　　我叫王红。　　____

男 女　　请你讲一下车祸发生的经过。　　____

男 女　　当时应该是他们那边的红灯。　　____

男 女　　但是他沒有停 ...　　____

男 女　　啊，他沒有停。　　____

男 女　　当时他的速度很快？　　____

男 女   对。   _____

男 女   有沒有失去知觉？   _____

男 女   这倒没有。   _____

男 女   还是去医院检查一下吧。   _____

男 女   那我现在怎么办？   _____

男 女   你有没有买保险呢？   _____

男 女   买了。   _____

男 女   请你把你保险卡拿出来让我看一看。   _____

男 女   喏，这是我（的）保险卡。   _____

男 女   我们会尽快跟你联系的。   _____

Now write six sentences (three that might be spoken by the male speaker and three by the female speaker) that each show a different one of these conversational functions. Using the numbers above, indicate which function it is. Try to use as much of the following vocabulary as you can: 单位，幸亏，受伤，冲，慌，安全带，突然，撞。

Example:

男：这辆车是你自己的吗？2 (asking for information)

1._____

2._____

3._____

4._____

5._____

6._____

 Follow-up Activities

大家来说 Role-playing (oral)

When Wang Hong got home that night she called her parents and told them what had happened. With a partner enact this conversation. Be sure to use the following vocabulary items: 幸亏，受伤，失去知觉，速度，冲过来，慌得很，撞，玻璃，闪开，系，流血，开不了，保险公司。

大家来写 Role-playing (written)

Imagine that you were a pedestrian who witnessed Wang Hong's accident. Using Chinese, write a paragraph describing in as much detail as possible exactly what you saw happen. Remember this will become part of the accident file so try to be precise.

_____

_____

_____

_____

_____

_____

_____

_____

_____

_____

_____

Lesson 32 (CD2.9) 第三十二课
A Tour of Universal Studios
参观环球影城

 **Preparation**

Useful vocabulary

旅行团	lǚxíngtuán	N	travel agency
游览	yóulǎn	V	to go sight-seeing, to tour
安排	ānpái	V	to arrange
集合	jíhé	V	to gather, to meet up, to assemble
纪念品	jìniànpǐn	N	souvenir
突然	tūrán	Adv	suddenly
盒饭	héfàn	N	box lunch (cf. 饭盒，便当)
地道	dìdào	Adj	genuine, authentic
行动	xíngdòng	N	movements, actions
老人家		N	elderly people
设施	shèshī	N	facilities
自动	zìdòng	Adj	automatic
电梯	diàntī	N	elevator
婴儿	yīng'er	N	baby, infant
寄存处	jìcúnchù	N	place to check things in

Imagine you are going to spend your holiday at Universal Studios (环球影城). On the next page is a map of its Studio Center. List five activities you would like to do when you are there.

1. 看看 Ron Howard 如何拍攝這部賣座電影，然後感覺現場溫度達一萬度的大火爆發場面！

First Alert 隆重推出

2. 看看我們的回到未來節目 (Back To The Future® Show) 背後的電子特殊效果是如何製造出來的，也看看影張大師希區考克 (The Magic of Alfred Hitchcock®) 的歷險刺激是怎麼來的，同時視目聽一下 Harry & The Hendersons Show 裡的音響效果

Kodak 隆重推出

3. 進去參觀電視喜劇第一皇后的事業歷程。

4. 快！跳上可以飛上星際的脚踏車！然後和 E.T. 一起飛到他的家，開始出乎想像的歷險，幫助 Cloud Bearers 和 Jumpums 拯救他們的星球。

AT&T 隆重推出

AT&T AT THE MOVIES

5. 一窗明目世界最峰造極的錄影區，觀眾可以參與其中。

*季節性節目

片廠設施

6. 片廠有軌遊覽車入口處
7. StarWay 電梯
8. 往娛樂中心的其他交通工具
9. 寄存嬰兒推車
10. 警衛處

 DINING

11. Studio Commissary
12. Soft Serve Shoppe
13. Margarita Bar
14. 點心停

 SHOPPING

15. Studio Store
16. E.T. Toy Closet*
17. E.T. Photo Spot*
18. Amazing Pictures
19. Lucy's Boutique
20. 電影*
21. Backdraft Souvenirs*

Listening for the Gist

The people who talked on the phone were …

	✓
a tourist and a bus driver.	
a tour guide and a tourist.	
the concierge at a hotel and a hotel guest.	
a travel agent and a tour guide.	

Did Mr. Wang already have some information about this tour? How do you know?

_____

_____

Who does Mr. Wang say he will go to Universal Studios with?

	✓
His wife.	
His son or daughter.	
His students.	
Some friends.	
His parents.	
A group of tourists from China.	

Listening for Details

Help Mr. Wang complete the following table based on what you heard on the CD:

Time	Place (no. on the map)	Activity
10:30 a.m.	#	
10:45 a.m.	#	
	#	
11:45 a.m.	#	
12:15 a.m.	#	

In English list three things Mr. Wang is concerned about regarding this tour:

1. _____

2. _____

3. _____

陈小姐提到了哪些设施？

设施	提到了	沒提到
饭馆		
电话亭		
电梯		
游览车		
婴儿车寄存处		
警卫处		

How did Ms. Chen translate the title of the movie *ET*? _____

What special attractions did she mention that pertain to the main character in this film?

_____

_____

旅行团为参加的人准备了什么？_____

要多少钱？_____

 ## Working with the Language

Fill in the blanks with one of the following phrases

一下　一类　一些　一起　一个　一张

1. _____地图　　　　5. _____小吃店

2. _____问题　　　　6. 跟我们_____去

3. _____影视效果　　7. 自动电梯_____的东西

4. 问_____

✳   ✳   ✳

Supply an object (in Chinese) for the following verbs based on what was said in this conversation. In some cases there may be more than one correct answer.

1. 问_____   6. 参加_____

2. 看_____   7. 存_____

3. 买_____   8. 准备_____

4. 坐_____   9. 帮助_____

5. 安排_____   10. 抱_____

Follow-up Activities

大家来说 Role-playing (oral)

Mr. Wang's mother got separated from the rest of her family in the crowded Star Way elevator. Could you tell her how to rejoin them? (Sorry, she does not speak English.)

大家来写 Role-playing (written)

Have you ever been to Universal Studios? If YES, write a guide for a group of students from China on an educational tour. If NO, write a description of the Studio Center according to the map. (Length: 50-100 Chinese characters.)

_____

_____

_____

_____

_____

_____

_____

_____

Lesson 33 (CD2.10)   第三十五课
On the Way to the Gym 去体育馆

 Preparation

Useful vocabulary

羽毛球	yǔmáoqiú	N	badminton
训练	xùnliàn	V, N	to train, training
比赛	bǐsài	V, N	to compete, competition
搭档	dādàng	V, N	to be partners, partner
专业	zhuānyè	Adj, N	professional, specialty; major
谦虚	qiānxū	Adj	to be modest
规则	guīzé	N	rules, regulations (cf. 规矩, 规定)
差	chà	Adj	inferior, poor, weak
		V	to differ, to lack
	chā	N	difference, discrepancy
爱好者	àihàozhě	N	fan (of sports, movie stars, etc.)
清惺	qīngxǐng	Adj	alert, wakeful
精力充分	jīnglì chōngfèn	Ph	full of energy
效率	xiàolǜ	N	efficiency, productiveness
彻底	chèdǐ	Adj	thorough
放松	fàngsōng	V	to relax, to be relaxed
按照	ànzhào	Prep	according to, on the basis of

Listening for the Gist

Check all the activities that Fang Ping and Wang Tao mention.

	✓
swimming	
badminton	
basketball	
soccer	
jogging	
bicycling	
pingpong	
tennis	
skiing	
ice skating	

What is the favorite sport practiced by each of the speakers?

Fang Ping	
Wang Tao	

What other topics are mentioned in this conversation?

	✓
Their personal experiences with professional athletic training.	
The importance of diet and nutrition for athletes.	
Their personal experiences with athletic competitions.	
Their interest in watching competitive sports.	
The benefits of exercise.	
How hard it is to find time to exercise regularly.	

Listening for Details

Based on the information in this conversation, complete these charts about Wang Tao and Fang Ping:

Wang Tao	
How often he practices.	
Name of his partner.	
Sport he learned as a child.	
Age he learned this sport.	
Who taught him?	
Types of training he received in China.	
Did he compete in China?	
If so, at what level?	
Who will organize upcoming competition?	
Will he participate?	
Other sports he regularly does.	

Fang Ping	
How often she does this sport.	
Age she learned this sport.	
Who taught her?	
Types of training she received in China.	
Did she compete in China?	
If so, at what level?	
Does she compete now?	
If so, at what level?	
Other sports she regularly does.	

What is Fang Ping's attitude toward soccer? Why?

_____

_____

What is Wang Tao's attitude toward the Chinese soccer team? Why?

_____

_____

Rearrange these phrases or sentences so that they are in the order they are spoken in the conversation and circle who the speaker is.

_____我才会觉得彻底放松。　　　　　王涛　　方萍

_____我做运动也是这个目的。　　　　　王涛　　方萍

_____运动完以后会觉得精力更加充分。　　王涛　　方萍

_____学习起来更有效率。　　　　　　　王涛　　方萍

_____我们现在学习这么紧张。　　　　　王涛　　方萍

_____让我的头脑更清惺一点。　　　　　王涛　　方萍

Working with the Language

Why does Fang Ping say "别谦虚"?

_____

_____

Think of a situation in which you might use this expression with one of your friends. Write this as a dialogue in Chinese below.

你的朋友：_____

你：　　　别谦虚！

＊　＊　＊

爱好者　　　fan: literally "one who is very fond of (sports/arts/movie stars, etc.)"

者　　　　　is a particle used in Classical Chinese that nominalizes what precedes it.

Consider these compounds. Can you match the Chinese with the English equivalents?

记者	scholar
学者	reader
作者	writer
读者	reporter

✴ ✴ ✴

Do you remember the context in which Fang Ping uses the expression 学习紧张 xuéxíjǐn-zhāng? Write a sentence with this phrase that relates to your own personal experience.

_____

✴ ✴ ✴

性　　xìng　　is added as a suffix to indicate -ty, -ness, -ility

In this conversation Fang Ping and Wang Tao spoke of sports competitions that were 全国性的. How would you translate this?

_____

Translate the following terms that have the suffix 性 added:

可能性 _____　　实用性 _____

科学性 _____　　可靠性 _____

创造性 _____　　社会性 _____

时间性 _____

Follow-up Activities

大家来说 **Role-playing (oral)**

That night Fang Ping's best friend from high school called from China. They had been on the swim team together for many years, and Zheng still swims competitively. Zheng was very curious about what kinds of sports Fang Ping is active in now, and Fang Ping is interested to hear about Zheng's experiences as a female athlete in China. With a partner, enact this conversation. Be sure to use at least the following vocabulary items: 训练，彻底，规矩，比赛，谦虚，专业，紧张，复杂，全国性的。

大家来写 **Role-playing (written)**

Here's a photo of Wang Tao and his teammates practicing badminton at the student recreation center. You are a reporter for the school newspaper and you have just been given the assignment of interviewing this team and discussing their upcoming competition. Write down eight to ten questions that you plan to ask them at this interview.

_____

_____

_____

_____

_____

_____

_____

_____

_____

Lesson 34 (CD2.11) 第三十四课
What a Coincidence! 真巧

 **Preparation**

Useful vocabulary

区	qū	N	district
课程	kèchéng	N	curriculum
博士(学位)	bóshì (xuéwèi)	N	Ph.D.
棒	bàng	Adj (Coll)	非常好,了不起 (liáobùqǐ)

Examples:

你研究中国的古典文学。你真棒。

这个电影很棒 。我真想再看一次。

硕士(学位)	shuòshì (xuéwèi)	N	Master's Degree
学位	xuéwèi	N	degree
如此	rúcǐ	Adj/Adv	like this, as such, in this way
巧	qiǎo	Adj	coincidental
结实	jiēshí	Adj	strong
印象	yìnxiàng	N	impression

Examples:

我对他印象很好。
I have a good impression of him.

这个电影给我留下了深刻的印象。
That movie left a deep impression on me.

Based on this section of a map of Beijing, see if you can locate the following places:

Beijing Train Station	北京站
Palace Museum	故宫博物馆
The Great Wall Restaurant	长城饭店
Tiān'ānmén Square	天安门
Cháoyáng Rd.	朝阳路
Cháoyáng District	朝阳区
Chairman Mao Memorial Hall	毛主席纪念堂
Tiāntán (Temple of Heaven) Park	天坛公园
Eastern City District	东城区
Tiāntán Hospital	天坛医院

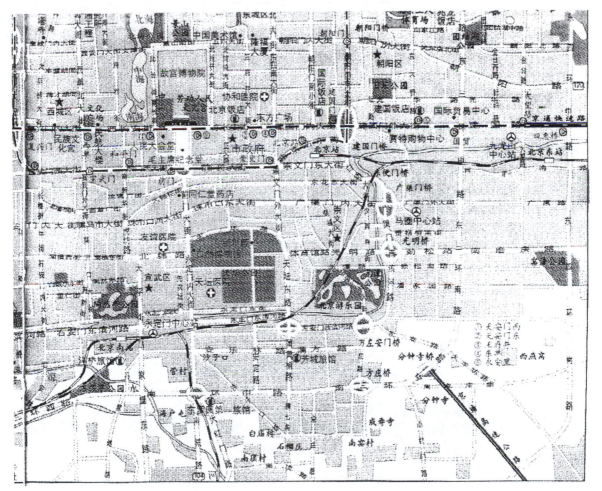

In meeting someone for the first time, what information would you expect to hear by way of introduction? How about if the person is from a foreign country? Jot down at least five things you might expect someone you are meeting for the first time to say or ask.

Listening for the Gist

Which topics were mentioned by the woman in this conversation?

	✓
Her name.	
Her occupation in China.	
Why she came to the the U.S.	
Her educational background.	
Location of her home in China.	
Location of her home in the U.S.	
Reference to any family members in China.	
Whether she has children.	
Her career plans.	
Her plans for further education.	

Toward the end of the conversation, the two speakers … (check all that apply)

	✓
exchanged phone numbers.	
exchanged email addresses.	
exchanged name cards.	
None of the above.	

Listening for Details

Based on the information given in this conversation, complete the chart.

Where Gao Língyù 高玲玉 is from.	
Her occupation in China.	
Her current occupation.	
How long she has lived in the U.S.	
Where she grew up (name of neighborhood).	
Relatives mentioned.	
Where Zhang Linsheng 张林生 is from.	
Where he grew up (name of neighborhood).	
His current occupation.	

What college did Zhang Linsheng attend?

	✓
Beijing University 北京大学 （北大）	
Beijing Normal University 北京师范大学 （北师大）	
Qinghua University 清华大学	
Beijing Industrial University 北京工业大学 (北工大)	

What college did Gao Lingyu attend?

	✓
北大	
北师大	
清华大学	
北工大	

Who is older? How do you know?

_____

_____

Why does he say that the two of them are 校友? What do you think this means?

_____

_____

What is the best translation for 我希望如此?

	✔
I hope so.	
I hope to do this.	
I hope you can do this.	
I hope I can be like you.	

Why does Gao Lingyu make this statement?

高玲玉说她将来要做什么？

	✔
找比较好的工作	
回中国教书	
在美国念硕士学位	
在美国念博士学位	

高玲玉为什么说他不太结实？这跟念书有什么关系？

_____

Check the expression Gao Lingyu says at the end of the conversation. Now circle the other expression(s) that is/are synonymous with her comment.

保持联络　　　保持健康

保持联系　　　保重身体

 **Working with the Language**

通 tōng is an extremely versatile verb that is used often in a range of contexts. The basic meaning is "to connect, to pass through". When 通 is duplicated it means "completely, thoroughly" (e.g., 北京的小地方他们通通知道). In this conversation Ms. Gao says, "我希望能夠通过硕士学位." What she means is that she hopes she can pass the exams (i.e., 硕士学位的考试) that will allow her to earn a Master's Degree. Can you figure out how 通 is used in these sentences? Translate each sentence into English.

1. 要是一个人说汉语，一个人说法文，他们的语言说不通。

_____

2. 那个小孩子一回家就跟父母通电話。

_____

3. 这条小路通吗？

_____

4. 高老师跟她的朋友每个星期通一次信。

_____

5. 新来的学生要通过语言考试才可以开始上课。

_____

6. 这个字不通用了。

_____

7. 那个小小的地方不通火车。

_____

8. 他学中文好几年了，一定是中国通。

_____

9. 你为什么不愿意去中国留学？我就想不通。

_____

10. 一个字怎么会有这么多用法，我通通不懂。

_____

Follow-up Activities

大家来说 Role-playing (oral)

With a partner imagine a situation in which you start talking to someone and then discover that you actually knew this person several years ago in a different place. Be sure to use at least the following vocabulary items: 真巧，世界真小，想不到，通，印象，好像，哪一天，聊一聊，保持联系。

大家来写 Role-playing (written)

That night Zhang Linsheng wrote an email message in Chinese to his classmate Li Wenying and told her about the way he ran into Gao Lingyu. What do you think he said in this message?

From: Zhangls@hotmail.com

To: Liwenying@yahoo.com

Subject: zhēnqiǎo

_____

_____

_____

_____

_____

_____

_____

_____

_____

_____

_____

_____

_____

Lesson 35 (CD2.12) 第三十五课
What's a "Typical" American?
典型的美国人

 **Preparation**

Useful vocabulary

恰恰	qiàqià	Adv	exactly
相反	xiāngfǎn	Adj	opposite
严谨	yánjǐn	Adj	strict, rigorous
试验	shìyàn	N	experiment
步骤	bùzhòu (bu zòu)	N	step, move
类似	lèisì	V	to be similar to
		Adj	similar, analogous
感受	gǎnshòu	V	to be affected by
		N	experience, feeling
创造力	chuàngzào lì	N	creativity
思维	sīwéi	N	thought, thinking
活跃	huóyuè	Adj	lively, animated (cf. huópo 活泼)
乐于	lèyú	V	to delight in, to take pleasure in
知音	zhīyīn	N	understanding friend, soul mate
典型	diǎnxíng	N	typical case, model;
		Adj	typical, representative
無法	wúfǎ	V O	unable to, not to have the means to
惊喜	jīngxǐ	N	pleasant surprise
		V	to be pleasantly surprised

How would you describe the typical American student? Do you think you fall into this category? Why or why not?

_____

_____

_____

_____

_____

_____

_____

 ## Listening for the Gist

Who has been in the U.S. longer?

    Wang Tao   Sun Xiaohua

Which of the following characteristics of American students were mentioned in this conversation?

	✓		✓
They are polite.		They are creative.	
They study hard.		They are enthusiastic.	
They like to party.		They are aggressive.	
They are very thorough.		They are independent.	
They like to exercise.		They are lively.	
They are friendly.			

Listening for Details

Complete the chart based on the information given in this conversation.

Wang Tao		Sun Xiaohua	
How long has he been in the U.S.?		How long has she been in the U.S.?	
What is his major?		What is her major?	

Before coming to the U.S., what did Wang Tao think American students were like?

_____

_____

After coming to the U.S., how did his impressions change?

_____

_____

What does Sun Xiaohua find most remarkable about the students in her Chinese class?

_____

_____

When trying to figure out what a typical American is like, who did Sun Xiaohua ask?
- ❑ A Chinese friend.
- ❑ One of the American students in her Chinese class.
- ❑ An American friend.
- ❑ One of the American teachers in the Chinese department.
- ❑ One of the Chinese teachers in the Chinese department.

Which of the following sentence(s) gives the same meaning as the comments made by the person who talked to Sun Xiaohua? (check all that apply)

- ❑ 我真的不能给你一个很正确的答案。

- ❑ 这个问题体很难，我沒办法回答。

- ❑ 我实在无法给你一个很准确的答案。

- ❑ 美国人的创造力非常强。

- ❑ 美国人要做什么就做什么。

- ❑ 美国人可以做他们心里想做的事。

- ❑ 每个美国人都不一样。

230

Did this person's explanation about "the typical American" make sense to Wang Tao? How do you know?

_____

_____

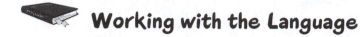 ## Working with the Language

Why does Sun Xiaohua say "你找到知音了"?

_____

What is another situation in which the term 知音 can be used? Write a brief dialogue in Chinese that you and one of your classmates might have in which you use this expression.

_____

_____

_____

_____

✳   ✳   ✳

力 can be used as a suffix to indicate strength, power, movement, or force. In this conversation Sun Xiaohua spoke of her student's 创造力. Do you remember what she said?

_____

_____

Consider these examples of 力 functioning in this way:

记忆力	jìyìlì	memory
说服力	shuōfúlì (PRC)	power of persuasion, persuasiveness
	shuìfúlì (TW)	
权力	quánlì	power, authority
功力	gōnglì	efficacy
重力	zhònglì	gravity
协力	xiélì	cooperation

Now see if you can figure out what the following terms mean (try not to use a dictionary!):

马力 _____ 能力 _____ 理解力 _____

酒力 _____ 笔力 _____ 药力 _____

 **Follow-up Activities**

 大家来说 **Role-playing (oral)**

With a partner discuss the ideas that Wang Tao and Sun Xiaohua mentioned about what a typical American student is. Do you agree with them? How would you describe the typical Chinese student? Do you think there are differences between students from the PRC and from Taiwan? Give examples to back up your opinions.

 大家来写 **Role-playing (written)**

After thinking further about this conversation, Wang Tao wrote a letter to a good friend in China who is planning to come study in the U.S. next year. He mentioned both what he himself had discovered about his American classmates as well as what he had learned from Sun Xiaohua and other friends. Help him write this letter. Be sure to use some of the new vocabulary from this lesson, such as 典型，感受，深刻，，创造，类似，乐于，知音，恰恰。

_____

_____

_____

_____

_____

_____

_____

_____

_____

_____

_____

_____

Lesson 36 (CD2.13) 第三十六课
Sightseeing in China 在中国遊览

 **Preparation**

Useful vocabulary

热闹	rènào	Adj	lively, buzzing with excitement
小吃		N	snacks
各地		N	(各个地方)
建议	jiànyì	V	to advise, to recommend
冰	bīng	N	ice
灯	dēng	N	lantern, lamp
雕	diāo	V	to carve
根本	gēnběn	Adv	basically, fundamentally

Have you traveled to China or thought about taking a trip there? If so, where did (or would) you go? What are some of the reasons why you would choose these places?

Have you ever lived in or visited a place that is very cold in the winter? What are some winter activities you associate with extremely cold climates?

_____

_____

Listening for the Gist

Which cities do Wang Tao and Sun Xiaohua mention in this conversation?

		✓
Beijing	北京	
Nanjing	南京	
Shanghai	上海	
Chengdu	成都	
Guangdong	广东	
Harbin	哈尔滨	
Xi'an	西安	

Which of them lived in northeastern China when young?

孙晓华   王涛

Listening for Details

Which places in Beijing does Sun Xiaohua say she has visited?

			✓
Summer Palace	颐和园	Yíhéyuán	
Temple of Heaven	天坛	Tiāntán	
Confucian Temple	孔庙	Kǒngmiào	
Fragrant Hill Park	香山	Xiāngshān	
Great Wall	(万里)长城	Chángchéng	
Tian'an men Square	天安门	Tiān'ānmén	

			✓
Wang Fujing St.	王府井	Wángfǔjǐng	
Great Bell Temple	大钟寺	Dàzhōngsì	
Palace Museum	故宫 (博物馆）	Gùgōng	
Beijing Zoo	(北京)动物园	Dòngwùyuán	
Beihai Park	北海公园	Běihǎigōng-yuán	
Ming Tombs	(明)十三陵	Shísānlíng	

Wang Tao says "不到长城非好汉." One way to translate this expression is:

❑ Someone isn't a good Chinese if they haven't been to the Great Wall.

❑ If you don't go to the Great Wall you won't like China.

❑ If you don't go to the Great Wall you can't be good at Chinese.

Where in Beijing does Wang Tao's family live?

_____

Most noteworthy thing mentioned about these places:

Xiang shan	
Wangfujing	
Chengdu	
Harbin	

Which of the speakers in this conversation likes to eat 麻辣火锅?

孙晓华   王涛

How cold does the temperature get in Harbin?

_____

Which of these words did Sun Xiaohua and Wang Tao use in this conversation when talking about the weather in different parts of China? (check all that apply)

	✓		✓
干燥		凉快	
潮湿		冷	
热		暖和	

Working with the Language

个 / 各   gè

It's easy to confuse 个 and 各 since both have the same pronunciation. Here are a few hints to keep in mind that will help you remember which one to use.

个 is often used as a non-specific measurement word.

个 is part of common words such as 个人 (individual), 个子 (stature, build) 个性 (gèxìng: personality or character).

各 often functions as a pronoun meaning "each" or "every" (e.g., 各有所好 hào each has his own likes [and dislikes]; 各有所长 cháng each has its strengths/strong points).

各 is also an adjective meaning "each" (e.g., 各式，各方面，各门课，各位).

各 is also an adverb meaning "separately" or "differently."

Note the difference:

各个	N	each, every
	Adj	one by one, separately
个个	N	each and every one, all

Circle whether 个 or 個 is appropriate in the following sentences.

1. 孙晓华愿意买 个/各 种好吃的东西。

2. 王涛的 个/各 子特别高。

3. 个/各 人喜欢吃的火锅不一样。

4. 在王府井大街可以买 个/各 式 个/各 样的小吃。

5. 每 个/各 人要参观的地方不同。

6. 个/各   位朋友，我们今天很高兴，请大家干杯。

7. 那 个/各 人的 个/各 性太强，很少有人要跟他去玩。

8. 个/各 地人去王府井一定要吃糖葫芦。

✳   ✳   ✳

Answer these questions according to the information given in this conversation and using the vocabulary item in parenthesis.

1. 孙晓华愿不愿意住在一个很冷的地方？

_____ （受不了）

2. 王涛小的时候喜欢玩什么？玩得怎么样？

_____ （根本）

＊　＊　＊

接著 + verb "to carry on, to continue"

Toward the end of this conversation, Sun Xiaohua said, "我们下次接著聊。" How would you translate this statement?

_____

List three other verbs that could be used in this way

接著_____

接著_____

接著_____

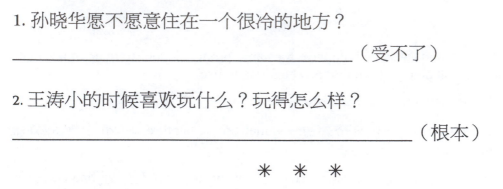

Follow-up Activities

大家来说 大家来写 **Role-playing (oral and written)**

With a partner plan a trip to China. What are some of the places you want to see, and how many days do you want to spend in each place? Refer to a map of China and write out and discuss your itinerary. Be as detailed as possible.

Reading

Here is a seven-day itinerary suggested by a travel agent in Beijing and some close-up maps of the Great Wall at Badaling, Fragrant Mountain Park, and the Ming Tombs. Answer the following questions based on these materials.

游程安排

第一天　游天坛、北海。

第二天　游八达岭长城、十三陵。

第三天　游香山、碧云寺、颐和园。

第四天　早上乘游 11 次火车去承德，游览外八庙。

第五天　游避暑山庄，午后乘游 12 次返京。

第六天　游天安门广场、毛主席纪念堂、故宫、景山。

第七天　商业区购物。

交通工具

北京 —火车→ 承德 —火车→ 北京

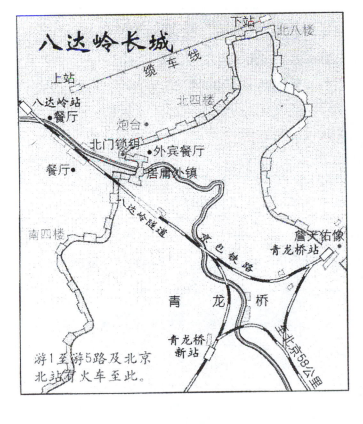

238

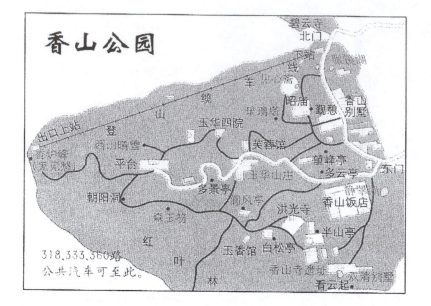

1. What other sight will be seen on the same day that you go to the Ming Tombs?

_____

2. Locate the Azure Dragon Bridge 青龙桥 at the Great Wall. What road is closest to it?

_____

3. What busses can you take to Fragrant Mountain Park?

_____

4. What three mountains are given on the map of the Ming Tombs?

_____

5. Which train will you take to Chengde 承德?

_____

6. Where in Fragrant Mountain Park is the Red Leaf Grove (红叶林) located?

_____

7. How many restaurants are there at the Great Wall at Badaling? Can you find them all?

_____

8. What will you do on Day 7?

_____

Lesson 37 (CO2.14) 第三十七课

Planning a Dinner Party 请客

 Preparation

Rewrite the Chinese characters under the appropriate picture.

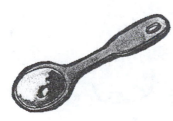

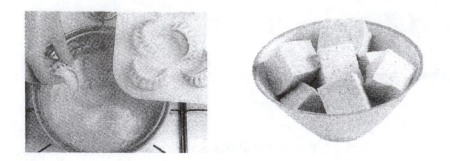

_____   _____

豆腐	大白菜	饺子
饺子皮	韭菜 jiǔcài	汤匙 tāngchí
姜 jiāng	茶匙	蘑菇 mógu (cf. 冬菇)
蔥 cōng	豆(腐)干 dòu(fǔ)gān	

Do you know what each of these ingredients is?

Write the English equivalent next to each item. Here's a list from which to choose: salt, pepper, frying oil, sesame oil, wine, soy sauce, vinegar, sugar, cornstarch, M.S.G.

Verbs + Objects

包饺子	bāo jiǎozi	to wrap *jiaozi*
擀皮	gǎnpí	to make the wrapping (also called "skin")
和面	huómiàn	to blend the flour, knead
拌馅	bànxiàn	to mix the stuffing (for the *jiaozi*)
调馅	tiáoxiàn	to mix the stuffing (for the *jiaozi*)

Additional useful vocabulary

去掉	qùdiào	V	to get rid of
紧	jǐn	Adj	tight, urgent
现成	xiànchéng	Adj	readymade

As you will hear in this conversation, Wang Tao (Sun Xiaohua's friend) is a connoisseur of Chinese teas. Here is a list of some of his favorite varieties. Write the corresponding letter and number for the pīnyīn and English equivalences.

		pīnyīn	English
c 4	龙井	a. júhuā	1. Jasmine
d 5	乌龙	b. xiāng piān	2. Chysanthemum
e 3	铁观音	c. lǒngjǐng	3. Iron Guanyin
b 1	香片	d. wúlǒng	4. Dragon Well
a 2	菊花	e. tiěguānyīn	5. Oolong

How many of these different types of tea have you tasted? Can you describe the flavor of each?

 **Listening for the Gist**

Why is Sun Xiaohua 孙晓华 so happy to see Wang Tao 王涛?

- ☐ She wants to ask him if he has any tea she could give her American friends.
- ☐ She wants to know where to buy ingredients for the food she is planning to cook at her dinner party.
- ☒ She wants to his advice about a dinner party she's planning.
- ☐ She wants to ask him to come to a dinner party.

Why is Sun Xiaohua worried? (check all that apply)

- ☐ She's not a very good cook.
- ☐ She's never entertained by herself before.
- ☐ She never made *jiaozi* before.
- ☐ She doesn't have a good recipe for *jiaozi*.
- ☐ She thinks her apartment is too small.
- ☐ She doesn't know how to wrap *jiaozi*.
- ☒ She doesn't know to make the stuffing for *jiaozi*.
- ☐ She doesn't know if she'll be able to make everything in time.

Listening for Details

Based on the information given, complete this chart:

Date of dinner party.	*SATURDAY*
Number of guests.	*5*
Time of dinner party.	*6:00*
Type of food they will eat.	*DUMPLINGS*
Type of tea to they will drink.	*DRAGON WELL*
Nationality of dinner guests.	*AMERICAN*

Which ingredients are used for the stuffing?

_____

How does Sun Xiaohua describe the *jiaozi* wrapping (饺子皮) she makes?

	✓
奇奇怪怪	
七手八脚	
奇形怪狀	✓
奇怪不像样	
乱七八糟	

What does Wang Tao think she must be doing wrong? (answer in English)

_____

_____

According to Wang Tao, what is the biggest mistake people make when they prepare the stuffing?

_____

According to Wang Tao, what is the biggest mistake people make when they prepare the wrappers?

_____

244

Based on the conversation indicate whether these statements are true (是) or false (非).

孙晓华跟王涛都是北方人。 是 ~~非~~

王涛愿意帮孙晓华的忙。 *yan* 是 非

王涛对做饺子非常有经验。 是 非

根据王涛的说法调馅的时候不能不放味精。 *MSG* 是 非

王涛说他会带一些很好的龙井茶。 是 非

孙晓华的美国朋友没喝过中国茶。 是 非

 ## Working with the Language

verb 来 verb 去 . . . "back and forth, over and over"

Toward the beginning of the conversation Sun Xiaohua said: "我想来想去，就觉得还是做饺子比较好。" How would you translate her statement?

_____

Complete the phrases below by adding one of the following expressions. (Hint: you might need to add a little more context to some of the sentences.)

走来走去　看来看去　想来想去　说来说去　找来找去

Example:

孙晓华不知道她把王涛的电话号码放在哪里。

↳ 孙晓华找来找去，可是找不到王涛的电话号码。

1.买菜的时候应该买什么样的肉。

_____

2. 忘了怎么翻译 "龙井茶。"

_____

3. 不记得那个卖中国菜的商店在哪条路。

_____

4. 不懂菜谱写的是什么。(càipǔ: cookbook)

_____

5. 沒告诉王涛她做过的饺子非常难吃。

_____

6. 书上没有一个孙晓华不认识的字。

_____

＊　＊　＊

Do you remember hearing these expressions in this conversation? If not, go back and listen again and see if you can figure out how they are used. Give a rough translation or para-phrase (in English) of the sentence or context in which these expressions occur.

取经

_____

_____

不怎么在行

_____

_____

犯错误

_____

_____

所以说

_____

_____

⇲ Follow-up Activities

大家来说 Role-playing (oral)

At the dinner party Sun Xiaohua's students talked about different kinds of Chinese food and tea that they had eaten and made before. With a partner enact one of these conversations. You might want to comment on some of the varieties of Chinese tea that Wang Tao brought for Sun Xiaohua's friends to try.

246

大家来写 **Role-playing (written)**

Here is another recipe for *jiaozi*. Circle the ingredients that were not listed in Wang Tao's recipe.

猪肉 (绞 jiǎo: ground TW; 肉馅 PRC)	半斤*
韭菜（或大白菜半斤）	四两
姜末	一茶匙
蔥花	一汤匙
酱油	一汤匙
酒	一茶匙
盐	一茶匙
蔴油	二汤匙
花生油	一汤匙

水铰的馅，可按各人喜好採用牛肉，羊肉，鸡肉或加入冬菇，虾仁，豆干，磨菇，芹菜等。

*一斤＝十两

According to the note given at the end of this list of ingredients, what else could be used instead of pork? (check all that apply)

	✓
shrimp	
lamb	
beef	
crabmeat	
turkey	
chicken	
fish	

What ingredients could be added (check all that apply)

	✓
scallops	
shrimp	
beancurd	
carrots	
green beans	
mushrooms	
celery	
spinach	

Lesson 38 (CD2.15) 第三十八课
Becoming a Father 初为人父

 **Preparation**

Useful vocabulary

Draw a line matching the characters to the appropriate parts of the face.

眼睛
耳朵
眉毛
鼻子
嘴巴

自从	zìcóng	Prep	since
哄	hǒng	V	to coax, to humor (children)
困	kùn	Adj	想睡觉
抱	bào	V	to hold, to carry
喂	wèi	V	to feed (milk) （cf. 喂奶 to nurse）
尿布	niàobù	N	diapers
代价	dàijià	N	price, cost
体重	tǐzhòng	N	weight
身高	shēn'gāo	N	height
扶	fú	V	to support with hands, to hold onto
討人喜欢	tǎorén xǐhuan		likable (lit. "demands that one likes [him/her]")
爹	diē	N	父亲，爸爸

Here is a picture of Zhang Linsheng and his newborn daughter.

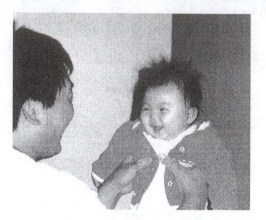

Imagine you are he and jot down what you might talk about if someone asked you what it's like to be a parent for the first time.

Listening for the Gist

In this talk the father mentions ... (check all that apply)

	✓
when the baby was born.	
what the baby is able to do.	
how the baby keeps the father busy.	
the financial cost of having a baby.	
how the baby pleases the father.	
his parents' reaction to having a granddaughter.	
the father's feelings about his baby.	
the sacrifices he has to make.	
a physical description of the baby.	

Check the word(s) that most appropriately fits the description of the father's feelings when he thinks of his daughter:

	✓
tired	
happy	
bittersweet	
angry	
loving	

Listening for Details

Complete these sentences that the father uses to describe his emotional state:

苦得_____，乐得_____。

Ever since the baby was born, the father has not ... (check all that apply)

	✓
gone to a movie.	
eaten a good meal.	
slept well.	
read a good book.	

In this monologue Zhang Linsheng uses the expression: 不当家不知柴米贵. The meaning of the saying is:

- ❑ You don't know how expensive rice and firewood are until you take charge of the cooking.
- ❑ You don't know how to cook unless you take charge of a family.
- ❑ You don't know how difficult it is to do something until you really do it.
- ❑ You don't know how costly things are until you have a child.

When the father says "真沒想到当爸爸要付这么大的代价," he means:

	✓
It is so expensive to buy clothing for his daughter.	
It is so costly to have a baby.	
The price of having children is too great to imagine.	
The price of being a father is really high.	

In what order does the father talk about the way his daughter looks?

鼻子	
眼睛	
眉毛	
嘴巴	
舌头	
头发	

The baby was taken to a doctor to have a health check. Please fill out the following chart:

姓名：	性別：	年齡：
身高：　　　　英寸	體重：　　　　磅	換尿布：　　次 / 天

能力：他（她）會不會做以下動作

❑ 微笑	❑ 大笑
❑ 說話	❑ "唱歌"
❑ 坐	❑ 站
❑ 爬	❑ 走
❑ 吃固體食物	❑ 翻身

Working with the Language

Imagine you are a father. If your child were to do the following, what would you do? (Use Chinese or write pīnyīn.) The first one has been done for you.

如果小孩...   爸爸要...

累了   要哄

饿了   _____

哭了   _____

醒了   _____

咳嗽了   _____

尿布湿了   _____

冷了   _____

渴了   _____

困了   _____

发烧了   _____

*   *   *

Respond to the following statements or questions based on what you think Zhang Linsheng might say. Be sure to use the patterns indicated in parentheses.

1.当爸爸有什么苦？

_____

（光是 ... 就）

2. 你女儿才四个月就会站了。是真的吗？

_____

（沒想到）

3. 既然当父亲这么苦，你就别当父亲了。

_____

（再+ verb）

Follow-up Activities

大家来说 **Role-playing (oral)**

Here are two photos taken when Zhang Linsheng's daughter was older. With a partner, discuss how she has changed and what changes you imagine have occurred in her relationship with her father.

大家来写 **Role-playing (written)**

Write out a telephone conversation between you and your parents about the reason(s) why you want or don't want to have children. Be sure that each speaker has at least 10-15 substantial lines of dialogue.

_____

_____

_____

_____

_____

_____

_____

Lesson 39 (CD2.16) 第三十九课
A Tragedy 惨剧

 **Preparation**

Useful vocabulary

引起	yǐnqǐ	V	to cause
评论	pínglùn	V	to comment on, to discuss
		N	commentary, critique, review
荣幸	róngxìng	N	honor
评论家	pínglùnjiā	N	critic, reviewer
预料	yùliào	V	to expect, to predict
具体	jùtǐ	Adv	concretely, specifically
吵架	chǎojià	V	to argue
惨	cǎn	Adj	tragic, miserable, disastrous
意外	yìwài	Adj	unexpected
行为	xíngwéi	N	behavior, conduct
寻找	xúnzhǎo	V	to seek
光明	guāngmíng	N	light
敏感	mǐn'gǎn	Adj	sensitive
异性	yìxìng	N	opposite sex
允许	yǔnxǔ	V	to allow
冲突	chōngtū	N	conflict
根源	gēnyuán	N	root, origin, basis

What are five things that you expect to hear in a news story about a celebrity murder case? (write in Chinese or English)

_____

_____

_____

_____

_____

_____

 Listening for the Gist

Who is Gu Cheng 顾城?

	✓
a movie star	
an athlete	
a poet	✓
a singer	
a politician	

256

Who did he kill?

	✓
his best friend	
his agent	
his girlfriend	
his wife	✓
his wife's lover	

Who is being interviewed? (check all that apply)

	✓
a literary critic	
a reporter	
Gu Cheng's lover	
Gu Cheng's friend	✓
a detective	
an actress	
a good friend of Gu Cheng's wife	

Listening for Details

The island Gu Cheng lived on is off the coast of …

	✓
Hainan.	
Taiwan.	
New Zealand.	✓
Hawaii.	

According to Ms. Chen, Gu Cheng had recently enjoyed what activities? (check all that apply)

	✓
fishing	
writing	
planting a garden	✓
getting together with friends	
designing a website	

Indicate whether the following statements are true (是) or false (非).

Ms. Chen hadn't talked to Gu Cheng in a long time. 是 *非*

Ms. Chen knew the news Thursday night. 是 *非*

Gu Cheng's older sister was at the scene of the crime. *是* 非

Gu Cheng killed his wife with a knife. *是* 非

Gu Cheng also killed himself. *是* 非

Ms. Chen had no idea why Gu Cheng would act in this way. 是 *非*

Listening to the interview, complete the lines of the poem Ms. Chen quoted. How would you translate these lines?

黑夜__给了我黑色的__眼睛；

__我去用它__寻找光明。

_____

_____

_____

What does Ms. Chen say about this couplet? Do you agree? Why? Why not?

_____

_____

_____

Put the radio announcer's comments in the order in which they were spoken during this interview.

_____今天我们节目的时间到了。

_____你能不能告诉我们当时的具体的情况呢？

_____我们再一次向陈小姐表示感谢。

_____今天我们荣幸地请到了著名评论家也是顾城的生前好友陈颖女士。

_____听说当时的情况非常惨。

_____这也是悲剧的根源。

_____大概沒有一个人会预料会有这样的事情发生。

按照陈小姐的说法，顾城跟他太太为什么吵架？

_____

_____

Working with the Language

Write the letter of the synonym or definition from Column B that corresponds to each expression in Column A.

Column A	Column B
＿＿＿ 如意	a. 太太
＿＿＿ 著名	b. 让
＿＿＿ 意外	c. 吵架
＿＿＿ 死去	d. 不会达到某种程度
＿＿＿ 口角	e. 沒想到
＿＿＿ 预料	f. 行为
＿＿＿ 允许	g. 事前推测
＿＿＿ 不至于	h. 有名
＿＿＿ 妻子	i. 去世
	j. 达到自己的愿望

✳ ✳ ✳

Which of these expressions were used in this interview in reference to Gu Cheng? (circle all that apply)

震惊	奇怪	敏感	疯了一样
悲伤	如意	生气	崇高的感情
冲动	漂亮	聪明	爱所有的异性
嫉妒	著名	不高兴	

How would you translate Ms. Chen's comment: 我不在场？

	✓
I wasn't on the scene.	
I'm not in that field.	
I'm not part of that group (of his friends).	

＊　＊　＊

Match the verbs to the objects that occurred with them in this interview. (**Note:** some verbs are used more than once.)

引起	光明
发生	意外
感到	消息
听到	评论
发表	惨剧
寻找	生命
	轰动

Follow-up Activities

大家来说 Role-playing (oral)

In a similar case, a woman named Song Yuying was arrested for killing her husband and his mistress. You and your partner are the defense lawyer and prosecutor. You are arguing the case in court.

大家来写 Role-playing (written)

Later Ms. Chen thought of another poem written by Gu Cheng. How would you read this poem in light of the comments given by Ms. Chen in this interview? See if you can translate it into English and then write a short paragraph in Chinese explaining how you interpret it.

感觉

天是灰色的

路是灰色的

楼是灰色的

雨是灰色的

在一片死灰中

走过两个孩子

一个鲜红

一个淡绿

Lesson 40 (CD2.17) 第四十课
Classical Chinese in the U.S.
"之乎者也"在美国

 **Preparation**

Useful vocabulary

文言文	wényánwén	N	Classical Chinese
理论	lǐlùn	N	theory
古典文学/现代文学		N	Classical/Modern literature
方式	fāngshì	N	way, style
角度	jiǎodù	N	angle, perspective
观点	guāndiǎn	N	point of view, standpoint
态度	tàidù	N	attitude, approach
交流	jiāoliú	V	to exchange
硕士	shuòshì	N	Master's Degree
博士	bóshì	N	Ph.D.
论文	lùnwén	N	thesis
尤其(是)	yóuqí (shì)	Adv	especially
之乎者也	zhīhūzhěyě	Ph	four classical particles that are used as a phrase to indicate pedantic language
虚字	xūzì	N	particles
掌握	zhǎngwò	V	to grasp

How many of these Chinese dynasties (cháodài 朝代) have you heard of? Jot down below what (if anything) you know about them or about premodern Chinese literature.

			✓
Zhōu	周	11th century-256 B.C.	
Qín	秦	221-207 B.C.	
Hàn	汉	206 B.C.-A.D. 220	
Táng	唐	618-907	
Sòng	宋	960-1279	
Yúan	元	1271-1368	
Míng	明	1368-1644	
Qīng	清	1644-1911	

Listening for the Gist

方萍是什么样的学生　　　　　几年级

❑　　大学生　　　　　❑　一　❑　二

❑　　研究生　　　　　❑　三　❑　四

Check which of these topics were mentioned in this conversation.

	✓
Differences in teaching methods in China and U.S.	
Difference in classroom dynamics in China and U.S.	
Specific areas of Chinese literature Fang Ping is studying.	
Fang Ping's favorite topics in Chinese literature.	
Why American students study Classical Chinese.	
The number of students in the class she helps teach.	
The materials students are reading in Classical Chinese.	
Wang Tao's opinion about studying Classical Chinese.	

Listening for Details

What is Fang Ping going to do when she runs into Wang Tao?

❑　　Go to the library to check out some materials.

❑　　Go to the library to return a book.

❑　　Go home to study.

❑　　Go home to grade papers.

❑　　Teach Classical Chinese.

❑　　Meet with students from her Classical Chinese class.

What does Fang Ping think is different about studying traditional Chinese literature in the U.S. versus studying it in China? (answer in English)

_____

_____

Match the type of literature that Fang Ping has studied with the dynasty that she mentions:

诗　shī　poetry　　　汉

词　cí　lyrics　　　元

赋　fù　rhapsody　　唐

　　　　　　　　　　宋

她写硕士论文的时候可能会选什么题目？

	✓
汉代的赋	
唐代的赋	
唐代的诗	
唐代的词	
宋代的诗	
宋代的词	
元代的词	
清代的诗	

Complete this chart:

Topic of the course Fang Ping is teaching	
Number of students in her class	
Other Chinese courses students are taking	
Are the students Chinese majors?	
How long the course has been in session	
What the students have learned so far	

What is Wang Tao's reaction when he hears that there are many American students studying Classical Chinese? Why?

_____

_____

Working with the Language

交流 jiāoliú   交换 jiāohuàn

Both these terms are verbs that mean "to exchange," but they are not interchangeable. 交换 usually refers to a more limited, one-time exchange or a swap, whereas 交流 expresses an ongoing process, usually involving abstract nouns such as ideas, experiences, or viewpoints. Which of these terms does Wang Ping use in conversation? Do you remember what she says? Write her sentence down here.

_____

Complete the following sentences using either 交流 or 交换 depending on the context.

1.圣诞节的时候有的人喜欢_____礼物。

2. 王涛今年是中国的_____学生。

3. 方萍愿意跟别的学生_____经验。

4. 这两个大学在教学上互相_____。

5. 方萍觉得他跟他的美国同学可以做思想上的_____。

*   *   *

到 ... 为止 "up to, as far as"

到 date or time expression 为止

到 a condition is met or a situation reached a certain result 为止

What does Fang Ping say has happened 到现在为止？

_____

Translate the sentences below that also use this construction:

1. 到现在为止，王涛还沒有很多机会跟美国学生來往。

_____

_____

2. 方萍昨天晚上在图书馆翻译汉赋。虽然她已经很累了，但他还坚持
(jiānchí: persist in, insist on) 到把整篇汉赋翻完为止。

_____

_____

3. 到目前为止，中文系的学生对学文言文一直很感兴趣。

_____

_____

＊　＊　＊

可 + verb = verb + able, can be verbed

Both Fang Ping and Wang Tao agree that the number of students in Fang Ping's classical Chinese course is a 可观的数目 (kěguānde shùmù: considerable or impressive number). Notice how adding the word kě before a verb turns that verb into an adjective (or stative verb), showing the potential mood (i.e., something can or is able to have that quality).

How would you translate these terms that consist of 可 + a verb? See if you can figure them out without looking at a dictionary.

可笑　_____　　可爱　_____　　可怕　_____

可口　_____　　可恨 hèn　_____　　可怜 lián　_____

可靠 kào　_____　　可信　_____　　可见　_____

可恥 chǐ　_____　　可惜 xī　_____　　可贵　_____

⇗ Follow-up Activities

大家来写 Role-playing (written)

Wang Tao decided to take Fang Ping up on her offer and visit her Classical Chinese course. He was quite surprised to discover that students were readings passages from *Lunyu* (the *Analects*) and were carefully learning the grammar of every line they read. After the class he decided to write an article about this group of American students learning Classical Chinese. He wanted to conduct the interview completely in Chinese. Help him think of five questions he could ask them and three questions he could ask the instructors. Write down the questions below:

Questions for the students

1. _____

_____

2. _____

_____

3. _____

_____

4. _____
_____

5. _____
_____

Questions for the instructors

1. _____
_____

2. _____
_____

3. _____
_____

大家来说 **Role-playing (oral)**

Using these questions, interview two or three students (in Chinese) who you know who are now studying Classical Chinese. Also, if possible, interview the instructor.

Now prepare a brief oral presentation on this topic, based on your interviews and based on the conversation between Wang Tao and Fang Ping.

Lesson 41 (CD2.18) 第四十一课
A Chinese Soap Opera 电视连续剧

 **Preparation**

Useful vocabulary

奋斗	fèndòu	V	to struggle
欢乐	huānlè	Adj	很高兴
移民	yímín	N	immigrant
破破烂烂	pòpòlànlàn	Adj	dilapidated, shabby
挣钱	zhèngqían	V O	赚钱
豪富	háofù	Adj	powerful and wealthy
大哥大	dàgēdà	N	cell phone (cf. 行动电话)
妙	miào	Adj	1. excellent, fine
			2. subtle, clever
空虚	kōngxū	Adj	void, emptiness，没有意义
孤单	gūdān	Adj	alone, 没有朋友
轰动	hōngdòng	V	to cause a sensation, to make a stir
矛盾	máodùn	N	contradiction; contradictory
遥远	yáoyuǎn	Adj	distant, remote
陌生	mòshēng	Adj	unfamiliar
恐惧	kǒngjù	N	fear, dread
冷淡	lěngdàn	Adj	cold, indifferent

What is a film you recently saw that has something to do with China or with Chinese people? Jot down the main plot and key characters and whether it involves universal themes such as issues of personal identity, family, or generational conflicts, etc. With a partner, discuss this film and its significance in Chinese.

_____

_____

_____

_____

_____

_____

_____

_____

Listening for the Gist

The people talking in this conversation are …

- ❑ two friends.
- ❑ a reporter and a writer.
- ❑ a television critic and an actor.

Which of the speakers has seen this television series?

	✓
the male speaker	
the female speaker	
both speakers	

This program they are discussing is about a …

	✓
New Yorker in Beijing.	
man from Beijing now living in New York.	
New Yorker who visited Beijing and returns to New York.	
man from Beijing who visited New York and returns to Beijing.	

Mr. Wang, the main character,…

	✓
is very poor.	
is very rich.	
starts out very poor and becomes wealthy.	
starts out wealthy and becomes very poor.	

In the television show Mr. Wang has a … (check all that apply)

	✓
wife.	
son.	
father.	
daughter.	
mother.	
niece.	

Where was this program originally shown on television?

_____

The TV show is very popular because people … (check all that apply)

	✓
like the main character (Mr. Wang).	
want to know about life in America.	
want to immigrate to the U.S. and become wealthy.	
want to know about the Chinese-American way of life.	
enjoy making fun of life in America.	

🔍 Listening for Details

Indicate whether the following statements are true (是) or false (非):

When Mr. Wang first arrives in New York, he …

speaks English very well.	是	非
has to do the hardest job.	是	非
has little money.	是	非
doesn't understand U.S. society very well.	是	非
has a friend who helps him considerably.	是	非

Check all Mr. Wang's experiences that are mentioned in this discussion of 北京人在纽约.

	✓
His successes	
His happiness	
His guilt	
His suffering	
His misfortunes	
His good luck	
When he made money	
When his parents died	
His marriage	
His divorce	
His failures	

When Mr. Wang first arrived in New York, what are some of the problems he faced?

	✓
他身体不好	
他不太会说英语	
他没有什么钱	
他太太离开了他	
他父母要他回中国去	

Complete the following sentences that describe what he did during those difficult times.

1. 他住在一个_____

2. 他去中国餐馆干最_____

3. 他常常被_____

The woman in this conversation says 深有同感. Do you think this comment is one of …

	✓
pity?	
empathy?	
ridicule?	
irony?	

How would you translate it?

_____

What are some of the ways Mr. Wang later demonstrated his success?

	✓
He bought an expensive car.	
He rented a huge apartment in Manhattan.	
He wore imported clothing.	
He owned a fancy house.	
He used a cell phone.	
He owned a state-of-the-art computer system.	
He entertained lavishly.	
He ran his own company.	

✻　✻　✻

Which of the following statement(s) would Mr. Wang probably disagree with? (**Note:** there may be more than one correct answer.)

1. 钱不能给一个人欢乐。　　　　4. 钱不能解决任何问题。

2. 有钱的人一定不幸福。　　　　5. 有很多钱不见得是一件好事。

3. 就是你有钱，你也可能会有别的问题。

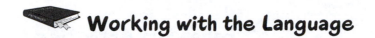 **Working with the Language**

Write the letter of the word from column B that is the closest antonym to each word in Column A.

Column A	Column B
_____ 陌生	a. 倒楣(霉)
_____ 成功	b. 充实
_____ 走运	c. 地狱
_____ 痛苦	d. 失败
_____ 天堂	e. 熟悉
_____ 冷淡	f. 失望
_____ 空虚	g. 欢乐
	h. 热情

Write the letter of the word from column B that is the closest synonym to each word in Column A.

Column A	Column B
_____ 欺负	a. 轰动
_____ 恐惧	b. 寂寞
_____ 发财	c. 干活
_____ 孤单	d. 好
_____ 一切	e. 怕
_____ 打工	f. 大钱
_____ 妙	g. 被别人骗
	h. 所有的

In the dialogue, the male speaker says: 他既没有钱，又不会说英语. What other sentence pattern beside 既 … 又 … could be used in this sentence that would express a similar meaning?

_____

_____

274

Follow-up Activities

大家来写 Role-playing (written)

Imagine an interview between a TV reporter and the actor who plays the role of Mr. Wang in this series. First write 5 to 8 thought-provoking questions that you would ask (in Chinese, of course).

1. _____

2. _____

3. _____

4. _____

5. _____

6. _____

7. _____

8. _____

大家来说 Role-playing (oral)

Now you are ready for the interview. Find a classmate who is willing to play the part of Mr. Wang and ask the questions you wrote above. Feel free to ask follow-up questions or to add your own comments in order to make the conversation flow naturally. If you run out of things to talk about regarding this particular TV show, imagine that this actor recently played a leading role in a Chinese film you and your partner have seen.

Lesson 42 (CD2.19) 第四十二课
Interviewing a Physically Disabled Student
访问残疾学生

 **Preparation**

Useful vocabulary

残疾	cánjí	N	disability
设施	shèshī	N	facilities
轮椅	lúnyǐ	N	wheelchair
通道	tōngdào	N	ramp
限制	xiànzhì	N	limitations, restrictions
障碍	zhàng'ài	N	obstacle
差异	chāyì	N	difference, discrepancy
缺陷	quēxiàn	N	shortcoming, flaw
激烈	jīliè	Adj	fierce, intense
技能	jìnéng	N	technical ability, mastery of a skill
草拟	cǎonǐ	V	to draft, to draw up

You are going to hear an interview with a student from China who has had polio since childhood. Jot down five concerns you think she might have about living and studying in the U.S.

_____

_____

_____

_____

_____

_____

_____

_____

 **Listening for the Gist**

Which of these issues were mentioned in the interview?

	✓		✓
transportation		financial losses	
education		personal struggle	
employment		physical therapy	
marriage		public facilities	
legal issues		daily life	

How would you describe the attitude of the woman being interviewed? What gives you this impression? (answer in English)

_____

_____

_____

What is your impression of the radio announcer? Why? (answer in English)

_____

_____

_____

Listening for Details

The name of the woman being interviewed is …

	✓
Wang Xiaoyin.	
Huang Xiaoyin.	
Wang Xiaoyan.	
Wang Xiaoying.	
Huang Xiaoying.	

How long has she been in the U.S.?

	✓
More than one month.	
More than two months.	
More than three months.	
Over half a year.	
A year.	
A few weeks.	

中国现在的残疾人有多少？

	✓
500,000	
5,000,000	
50,000,000	
500,000,000	

为了解决在外面上厕所的困难，有的残疾人…

	✓
穿上成人用的尿布	
先吃一点药	
出门之前不喝水	
整天呆在家里	

小英提到，在中国进入大学之前要经过…

	✓
老师介绍	
身体检查	
学科考试	
政治审查	

大部分在中国的残疾人只能做的工作是

	看门	打字	教学	听电话	做衣服	收报纸
✓						

小英来美国念的是

	大学一年级	大学四年级	硕士学位	博士学位
✓				

节目主持人说小英是"自学成才。"小英自学的是

	外语	图书馆学	新闻学	电子工程
✓				

In which country does Xiaoying find these problems more serious?

	中国	美国
沒有残疾人洗手间		
沒有家人的照顾		
沒有轮椅通道		
沒有免费医疗		
沒有大学接受她		
沒有图书馆和宿舍		

What does the Xiaoying say she intends to tell her friends with disabilities back in China?

_____

_____

_____

Working with the Language

Do you remember the meaning of each of these compounds with 专 zhuān? See if you can translate each below. Which of these compounds with 专 did you hear in this conversation? Circle each term.

专业_____ 专用 _____ 专门_____

专心_____ 专家_____ 专长_____

* * *

Which of these expressions can be used to introduce examples or offer clarification?

譬如 pìrú   看样子   例如 lìrú   举例来说   对于

比如   另一方面   像   这样   比方说   就是说

* * *

相当(于)   V   to correspond to, to be equal to (cf. 等于，跟 . . . 一样)

　　　　　Adj   suitable, appropriate

　　　　　Adv   considerably, quite

In this interview the host of the radio show (节目主持人) and Xiaoying both use the term 相当 several times. Circle who said which of these comments.

相当的不简单！ 节目主持人 小英

拿到了相当于大学毕业的文凭。 节目主持人 小英

那相当好。 节目主持人 小英

Now rewrite each of the following sentences using 相当.

1. 小英认为他有非常多机会。

_____

2. 她总是觉得他挺幸运。

_____

3. 按照她老师的说法，在高中学三年的英文跟在大学学一年的英文一样。

_____

_____

4. 在中国很多残疾人找不到合适的工作。

_____

✻ ✻ ✻

Write the letter of the synonym or definition from Column B that corresponds to each expression in Column A.

Column A	Column B
____ 必须	a. 生活上的问题多
____ 发挥 fāhuī	b. 不收钱
____ 就业	c. 行动
____ 困难	d. 分别
____ 摁 èn	e. 不方便
____ 审查 shěnchá	f. 把内在的能力表现出来
____ 免费 miǎnfèi	g. 用手按

Column A	Column B
____ 不便	h. 得到工作
____ 差异	i. 一定要
	j. 仔细检查

＊　＊　＊

Write the letter of the antonym from Column B that corresponds to each expression in Column A.

Column A	Column B
____ 减少 jiǎnshǎo	a. 倒楣
____ 安全	b. 长处
____ 幸运 xìngyùn	c. 难过
____ 缺陷	d. 危险
____ 愉快 yúkuài	e. 增加
	f. 快乐

 **Follow-up Activities**

 大家来说 **Role-playing (oral)**

Later that month Xiaoying was planning to travel from Denver to Richmond, Virginia to visit some friends who live there. She will need to change planes either in Washington D.C. or Chicago. She has decided to talk to the customer-assistance specialist at O'Hare International Airport and the one at Dulles International Airport to find out about how she'll be able to manage her luggage and transfer to the second flight and how long a layover there will be between flights. She's also concerned about the facilities available at each airport, especially if she needs to eat a meal or buy some gifts for her friends. Help her enact these phone conversations so she can make the best decision.

Reading

Recently the Chinese government sent out a survey (调查 diàochá) to all physically disabled students. Please help Xiaoying complete this form. First answer some short questions that will give you some helpful hints about some of the vocabulary in the survey that may be unfamiliar.

1. A translation of the heading of this survey is

_____

2. In this questionnaire, what do the instructions 可选择多项 mean?

- ❏ You can choose multiple items.
- ❏ There are many choices for disabled people.
- ❏ Disabled people are often allowed to choose many topics.

3.建筑 jiànzhù (jiànzhú) as a verb means "to construct, to build." As a noun it means "construction, building, structure." It also means "architecture." What do you think 建筑物 means in this context?

_____

Now you are ready to complete the questionnaire according to the information you heard in the interview.

關於殘疾人保障法的調查

姓名：_____   性別：　　男　　　女

年齡：　　21-35　　　　　36-50　　　　　50以上

工作單位：_____

教育程度：　☐ 小學畢業　　☐ 初中畢業　　☐ 高中畢業
　　　　　　☐ 中專畢業　　☐ 大專畢業
　　　　　　☐ 大學畢業或同等學歷

我國政府正在草擬殘疾人保障法，請你提意見。

一、殘疾人的權利應在哪些方面得到保障？（可選擇多項）
　　　☐ 受高等教育的機會　　☐ 就業機會
　　　☐ 房屋分配　　☐ 交通服務

二、你認為新的建築物應該規定有哪些設施？
　　　☐ 殘疾人保健室　　☐ 自動售貨機　　☐ 遙控門*
　　　☐ 殘疾人洗手間　　☐ 自動門　　　☐ 輪椅通道
　　　☐ 小型摩托車**專用道　　☐ 電暖爐　　☐ 電梯

謝謝！

* remote control gate　　　　　　** scooter

大家来写 Role-playing (written)

After this interview Xiao Ying wrote a letter to close friend in China who is also physically disabled. In this letter she wrote about her current experience as a student in the U.S. Be sure to mention specific differences between handicapped students in the U.S. and in China, and also your interactions with American students. (This letter should be 80-120 Chinese characters long).

_____

_____

_____

_____

_____

_____

_____

_____

_____

_____

_____

_____

_____

_____

_____

_____

_____

_____

Lesson 43 (CD2.20) 第四十三课
Cultural Differences 华裔美人

 **Preparation**

Useful vocabulary

陆续	lùxù	Adv	in succession, one after another (陆陆续续地)
冲击	chōngjǐ	N	clash, conflict
如何	rúhé	Adv	how (cf. 怎么)
取舍	qǔshě	V	to accept or reject, to make one's choice
综合	zōnghé	V	to synthesize, to blend
传授	chuánshòu	V	to pass on, to teach, to impart
以 … 为荣	yǐ … wéiróng		to take X as an honor
严格	yángé	Adj	strict, rigorous
幼儿所*	yòu'ér suǒ	N	kindergarten (*Ms. Li meant to say 托儿所 tuō'ér suǒ; cf. 幼稚园 TW; 幼儿园 PRC)
灌输	guànshū	V	to teach, to inbue with, to instill
血統	xuètóng	N	blood relationship, lineage
(考试)卷子	juànzi	N	test paper
生成	shēngchéng	V	to be born

A Chinese friend of yours is describing to you her experience of raising her children in America. Think about the types of conflicts that parents might face when their children grow up in a culture different from the one in which they grew up. Jot down five examples.

_____

_____

_____

_____

_____

_____

_____

 **Listening for the Gist**

Of the following topics, check all that you heard her talk about:

	✓
Her name.	
Her background.	
How long she has been in the U.S.	
Names of her children.	
Her goals in raising her children.	
Chinese popular music.	
American popular music.	
Studying Chinese language.	
Her children's friends.	
Listening to the radio.	
Advice she gives her children.	
Difficulties her children face in being both Chinese and American.	

How many Chinese sayings does she quote toward the end of her comments?

一　　　　　二　　　　　三　　　　　四

Listening for Details

Complete this chart based on what you heard in this monologue.

	✓
Her name (give pinyin)	
Number of children	
Ages of children (specify which one[s])	
How long she has been in U.S.	
Where she is from	
Grades her children are in	

Select the phrase that best completes each of the following sentences based on what the speaker said.

她三个孩子一定要 ...

	✓
学会如何说中文，看中文，写中文。	
每天吃中国菜，也要学会怎么做中国菜。	
将将来住在台湾。	
多交一些中国朋友。	

她跟她老大开车去 ...

	✓
超级市场	
中文学校	
朋友家	
购物中心	

她说西方的社会…

	✓
是不容易了解的。	
比较注重自我。	
比较注重钱。	
不太注重教育。	

她觉得最大的难题是 …

	✓
不知道应该用什么方法教育孩子。	
强迫孩子学中文。	
孩子们对中国社会沒有兴趣。	
如何劝孩子跟中国人结婚。	

她的儿子为什么把收音机关掉了？(请用中文回答)

_____

Ms. Li refers to a couple of frequently used Chinese sayings toward the end of her monologue. The first is: 覆巢之下无完卵 fù cháo zhī xià wú wán luǎn (覆巢无完卵), which literally means "if the nest is overturned there won't be any whole eggs left." Which of the following are extended meanings of this expression? (check all that apply)

- ❑ In a total disaster no one will survive.
- ❑ If a country is defeated, all its people will suffer.
- ❑ If chaos occurs, only the strong will survive.
- ❑ Sometimes it's better to abandon a sinking ship.
- ❑ People with experience will be needed in times of trouble.

How does it relate to what she's talking about here?

_____

The second saying she mentions is: "我走过的桥比你吃的饭还要多。" Unfortunately she actually confused two different sayings, which are: (1)"我走过的桥比你走过的路还要多" and (2) "我吃过的盐比你吃过的饭还要多。" How would you translate these sayings?

1. _____

2. _____

How do you think you might react if your parents or someone older than you said one or both of these phrases to you? Why?

_____

Working with the Language

Fill in a letter in the second column to match the words in column A with the word or phrase with the same or similar meaning in column B.

Column A	Column B
_____ 缺点	a. 严格
_____ 传授	b. 长处
_____ 难题	c. 不知道
_____ 取舍	d. 不容易解决的问题
_____ 收音机	e. 把技艺教给别人
_____ 优点	f. 短处
_____ 不晓得	g. 要或不要
	h. 听广播的机器

✳ ✳ ✳

Below is a paragraph Ms. Li wrote in a letter to a friend once when she was thinking about this same topic. Fill in the blanks with words from the following list. Not all the words will be used.

传授　　文化　　陆续

了解　　比较　　教育

自我　　交　　感受

差异　　严格　　传统

我从小受的是中国的_____。但是我孩子所接触的

_____完全是西方的，_____的也都是西方的朋友。我觉得西方社会

_____注重_____，而中国人会更多地想到别人需要或_____。我

希望我的孩子多_____中国文化和西方文化在这方面的_____。

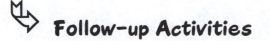 **Follow-up Activities**

 大家来说 **Role-playing (oral)**

Find a partner and talk about the times when your parents embarrassed you. Did these events mainly occur because of cultural differences between you and your parents or because of generational differences? Be sure to give specific examples.

大家来写 **Role-playing (written)**

Imagine that you are this woman's son or daughter. Write a letter to a friend explaining how you feel about growing up as a Chinese American. Try to include the following vocabulary: 态度，严格，优点，观念，教育，要求，以 ... 为荣，注重，传统，综合。

_____

_____

_____

_____

_____

_____

_____

_____

_____

_____

_____

_____

_____

Lesson 44 (CD2.21) 第四十四课
It's Hard to Be a Mother! 母亲难为

 **Preparation**

Useful vocabulary

圆桌	yuán zhuō	N	round (shaped) table
共享	gòngxiǎng	V	to share, to enjoy together
土生土长	tǔshēng tǔzhǎng	Ph	locally born and bred
融合	rónghé	V	to mix together, to blend
同样	tóngyàng	Adv	equally, similarly
(不)仅仅	bùjǐnjǐn	Adv	(not) merely, (not) only
期望	qíwàng, qīwàng	N	希望
苛责	kēzé	V	to criticize severely
多余	duōyú	Adj	excessive, uncalled for, unnecessary
鼓励	gǔlì	V	to encourage
铺床	pūchuáng	V O	to make a bed
盖章	gài (yige) zhāng	V O	to affix a stamp
及格	jígé	V	to pass a test (不及格, to fail a test)
自信心	zìxìnxīn	N	self-confidence
自尊心	zìzūnxīn	N	self esteem

Listening for the Gist

Which of these topics does the speaker mention in this talk?

	✓
Why she went to Taiwan.	
Where she stayed.	
Ages of her children.	
Her childrens' table manners.	
Table manners of people who live in Taiwan.	
Expectations of teachers in the U.S.	
Expectations of teachers in Taiwan.	
Expectations of Chinese parents.	
Expectations of American parents.	
Chinese students' sense of responsibility.	
American students' sense of responsibility.	
Her hopes for her children.	
Her hopes for herself.	

Listening for Details

Complete this chart based on what you heard in this monologue:

How long did Ms. Li stay in Taiwan?	
How many children did she bring with her?	
What did they do?	
Where did they live?	
Why did she take her children there?	
What gender are her children?	
What are the ages of her children?	

Explain some of the cultural differences Ms. Li mentioned in these situations (write your answer in English):

Eating at a friend's home	
Eating *jiaozi* at a restaurant	
Taking a spelling test in the U.S.	

What does Ms. Li mean when she says that Chinese people often "观察别人的脸色"? Do you think Americans do this too?

_____

What were some of Li Yinghui's responsibilities when she was a student? (check all that apply)

- ❑ Make her bed.
- ❑ Clean her room.
- ❑ Help cook dinner.
- ❑ Do well in her schoolwork.

Answer the following questions in Chinese.

1. 根据李小姐的说法，中国人吃饭的时候为什么不会把菜吃光？

_____

_____

2. 她为什么觉得，刚来美国的时候，自己这么不能干？

_____

_____

3. 李小姐认为美国的孩子养成了什么坏习惯？

_____

_____

 # Working with the Language

主义

What does the speaker of this monologue say about 自我主义? Write down the context in which she uses this term.

_____

The suffix 主义 zhǔyì means "theory" or "doctrine" and is added to many words to mean "-ism," as in 自我主义, egoism.

Match the following terms:

马克思主义	impressionism
社会主义	feminism
资本主义	anarchism
国际主义	fatalism
共产主义	socialism
印象主义	individualism
女权主义	capitalism
民族主义	Marxism
无政府主义	nationalism
个人主义	communism
	internationalism

✳ ✳ ✳

Here are a few of Ms. Li's comments, but some of the words are missing. See if you can fill in the blanks without listening to the monologue. Then check to see if you are right by playing the audio segment again.

教育	根本	不仅	为	对
期望	答对	不及格	带	共享

1. 像念书一样，这里念书都是_____你自己，可是在台湾你_____是_____自己念书。你念书的时候还_____著你家里人_____你的_____。

2. 在中国的_____里面，你十二个里面只_____了六个，那个_____就是_____的。

Now go back and translate these sentences into English.

_____

_____

_____

_____

Follow-up Activities

Reading

Here's Li Yinghui's ID card from Taiwan. Answer the following questions based on the information on this card.

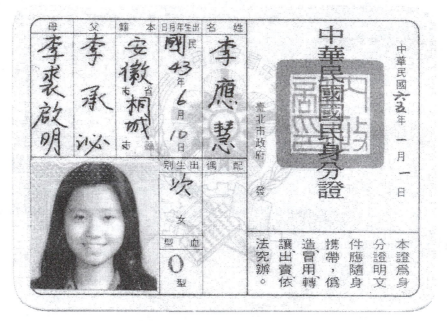

What are her parents' names?

_____

When was she born? (Do you remember how dates are indicated in Taiwan?)

_____

What is her blood type?

_____

When was this card issued?

_____

What is her 本籍 (běnjí: ancestral native place)?

_____

Here is a table comparing the number of days that students in various countries are required to attend school.

Country			Length of School Year in Days
中国			251
日本			243
韩国	Hánguó	Korea	220
以色列	Yǐsèliè	Israel	215
德国	Déguó	Germany	210
俄国	Éguó	Russia	210
瑞士	Ruìshì	Switzerland	207
荷兰	Hélán	The Netherlands	200
苏格兰	Sūgélán	Scotland	200
泰国	Tàiguó	Thailand	200
美国			180

When Ms. Li saw this chart, she became even more concerned about the current problems in American education. With a partner, imagine that she is discussing this situation with one of her children's teachers.

大家来写 **Role-playing (written)**

Write a short narrative in Chinese from the perspective of one of Ms. Li's children describing the incident she described involving Chinese vs. American table manners.

_____

_____

_____

_____

_____

_____

_____

Lesson 45 (CD2.22) 第四十五课
On Revolutionary Song 革命歌曲

 **Preparation**

Useful vocabulary

热潮	rècháo	N	upsurge
怀旧	huáijiù	V	to yearn for the past
传统	chuántǒng	Adj, N	traditional, tradition
现象	xiànxiàng	N	phenomenon
志愿军	zhìyuànjūn	N	volunteer army
牺牲	xīshēng	V, N	to sacrifice, sacrifice
事迹	shìjī	N	a person's lifetime accomplishments
抒情	shūqíng	Adj	lyrical
		V O	to express one's emotions
高昂	gāo'áng	Adj	exalted, elated
咬字	yǎozì	V O	to "over-enunciate" lyrics, an operatic technique in which the singer exaggerates the lyrics
摇滚乐	yáogǔnyuè	N	rock 'n roll
符合	fúhé	V	to accord with
反映	fǎnyìng	V	to reflect
怀疑	huáiyí	V, N	to suspect, to doubt; suspicion, doubt
分析	fēnxi, fēnxī	V, N	to analyze, analysis

Additional vocabulary

Match these words to the corresponding English meanings.

_____	乐器	a. solo
_____	歌词	b. to give an instrumental performance
_____	炮声	c. singing style
_____	乐队	d. singer, vocalist
_____	歌手	e. to sing in performance
_____	演唱	f. musical instrument
_____	女高音	g. main theme
_____	主题	h. lyrics
_____	独唱	i. sound of artillery
_____	唱法	j. orchestra, band
_____	演奏	k. soprano

In Communist China, politics became all-powerful. The Central Philharmonic Society, established in Beijing in 1956, was urged to play even more Chinese pieces ... Mao Zedong had denounced art for art's sake. "All culture or literature and art belongs to a definite class and party, and has a definite political line."

— *New Asia Review*, charter issue (1994): 28.30

The so-called "revolutionary song" you are about to hear was actually a patriotic piece, in contrast to the internationalism in its French counterpart, *L'internationale*. This song was written to praise a soldier of the Liberation Army, who died on the battlefield, as a national hero.

Before listening to the audio segment, circle the characteristics that you think might be typical of a Chinese revolutionary song:

Tone	Tempo	Theme	Image	Main Instruments
sorrowful	very slow	internationalism	lovers	flute
satirical	slow	humanism	soldiers	piano
lyrical	quick	patriotism	intellectuals	harp
majestic	very quick		bourgeouisie	drum

Listening for the Gist

In this program the radio announcer did **not** …

	✓
give historical background for the songs.	
make a comparison between the songs.	
mention the name of the hero's sister.	
mention the singers' names.	

The relationship of the first song to the second is …

	✓
the same song sung in a different dialect.	
a traditional versus a modern adaptation.	
a different version sung by the same singer.	
the same music with different lyrics.	
There is no relation between the two songs.	

As you listen to these songs identify which has these characteristics:

	Song #1	Song #2
50s/60s		
rock		
female singer		
clear pronunciation		
playful tone		
husky voice		
jazz		

Listening for Details

Match each of the specific items on the right to the general topics on the left:

name of the radio program	文化大革命
name of the movie	你唱我唱大家唱
hero of the story	英雄儿女
a historical event	抗美援潮战争
	王成

Based on this radio program, determine if the following statements are true (是) or false (非):

重唱革命歌曲是中国近几年来的一股怀旧热潮。   是   非

《英雄儿女》 是七十年代的小说。   是   非

王成在战争中牺牲了，他的妹妹王芳也牺牲了。   是   非

歌手受过传统的音乐训练。   是   非

第二首歌反映了现代年轻人对共产主义怀疑的态度。   是   非

勇士腐烂变泥土，敌人辉煌化金星。   是   非

Working with the Language

Answer the following questions in Chinese based on what was said in this radio program, using the words or expressions in parentheses in your answer.

1. 革命曲跟中国七十年代的社会有什么关系？

_____

（反映）

2. 根据这位节目主持人，传统的唱法跟现代的唱法有什么不同？

_____

（保持）

3. 第一首歌和第二首歌的歌词跟音乐有差别吗？

_____

（符合）

4. 如果你不同意节目主持人这样分析这两首歌曲，你可以做什么？

_____

（同样时间）

＊　＊　＊

一向，甚至，总之

Do you remember hearing these expressions in the radio broadcast? If not, go back and listen again and see if you can figure out how they are used. Give a rough translation or paraphrase (in English) of the sentence in which these expressions occur.

一向

_____

_____

甚至

_____

_____

总之 (abbreviated form of 总而言之)

_____

_____

Now fill in the blanks following sentences with the appropriate one of these expressions and then translate each sentence into English.

1. 现在住在大陆的中国人_____认为革命曲是当代中国历史的一部分。

_____

2. 很多年轻人觉得国歌对自己，对父母，_____对祖宗，都有相当大的的意义。

_____

3. _____他们以这类的音乐为重要的研究项目。

_____

⇨ Follow-up Activities

大家来说 Role-playing (oral)

With a partner, imagine that one person is a disc jockey and the other is a listener who is calling in to request a song. Be sure to discuss your individual preferences in music, such as favorite performers, composers, and styles of music, and be prepared to defend or explain your choices.

大家来写 Role-playing (written)

Fill in the lyrics based on what you heard in this program. A list of words from which you can choose is given below. Some words may be used more than once.

地　血　花　为　鲜　大　么　开　什

_____ _____ _____战旗美如画？

英雄的_____ _____染红了它。

为什么_____ _____春常在？

英雄的生命_____ _____ _____。

Now translate this stanza into English:

_____

_____

_____

_____

VOCABULARY INDEX 生詞表

bǎoxiǎn	保險	保险	31
bǎozhòng shēntǐ	保重身體	保重身体	8
bào	抱	抱	38
běi	北	北	1
běnjí	本籍	本藉	44
bízi	鼻子	鼻子	38
bǐjiào(jiǎo)	比較	比较	12
bǐsài	比賽	比赛	33
bǐlì	筆力	笔力	35
bìyè	畢業	毕业	2
biānjí(jì)	編輯	编辑	17
biàndāng	便當	便当	32
biànhuà	變化	变化	22
biāozhì	標誌	标志	26
bīng	冰	冰	36
bōlí	玻璃	玻璃	31
bózi	脖子	脖子	30
bóshì(xuéwèi)	博士（學位）	博士（学位）	34, 40
búguò	不過	不过	25
bú (yòng)kèqile	不（用）客氣了	不（用）客气了	3
bú (yòng)xièle	不（用）謝了	不（用）谢了	3
bùduōjiǔ	不多久	不多久	14
bùjígé	不及格	不及格	44
(bù)jǐnjǐn	（不）僅僅	（不）仅仅	44
bùzěnme zàiháng	不怎麼在行	不怎么在行	37
bùxíng	步行	步行	26

bùzòu	步驟	步骤	35

C

cáiliào	材料	材料	14
càipǔ	菜譜	菜谱	37
cánjǐ	殘疾	残疾	42
cǎn	慘	惨	39
cǎonǐ	草擬	草拟	42
cè	側	侧	26
chá	查	查	13
chá zìdiǎn	查字典	查字典	13
chá	茶	茶	5
cháchí	茶匙	茶匙	37
chà(chā)	差	差	33
chà(chā)buduō	差不多	差不多	30
chà(chā)yì	差異	差异	42
chà(chā)yìdiǎn(r)	差一點兒	差一点儿	30
chāi fángzi	拆房子	拆房子	22
cháng(yìcháng)	嚐（一嚐）	尝（一尝）	29
chángshòu	長壽	长寿	15
chàngfǎ	唱法	唱法	45
chènshān	襯衫	衬衫	9
chāozhòng	超重	超重	23
cháoshī	潮濕	潮湿	10
chǎojià	吵架	吵架	39
chēwèi	車位	车位	18
chèdǐ	徹底	彻底	33

chīsù	吃素	吃素	12
chídào	遲到	迟到	10
chōngjī	沖擊	冲击	43
chōngjì	沖劑	冲剂	30
chōng	衝	冲	31
chōngtū	衝突	冲突	39
chōuyān	抽煙	抽烟	23
chūfā	出發	出发	27
chūzūqìchē	出租汽車	出租汽车	11
chūqī	初期	初期	30
chuán	船	船	11
chuánshòu	傳授	传授	43
chuántǒng	傳統	传统	45
chuánzhēnjī	傳真機	传真机	23
chuàngzào	創造	创造	29
chuàngzàolì	創造力	创造力	35
chūnjià	春假	春假	11
chūnjié	春節	春节	12
chūntiān	春天	春天	10
cí	詞	词	40
cōng	蔥	葱	37
cónglái bù/méi	從來不沒	从来不没	10

D

dādàng	搭檔	搭档	33
dáduì	答對	答对	44
dǎ bàngqiú	打棒球	打棒球	20

dǎ lánqiú	打籃球	打篮球	20
dǎ pīngpāngqiú	打乒乓球	打乒乓球	20
dǎrǎo	打擾	打扰	28
dǎsǎn	打散	打散	29
dǎsuàn	打算	打算	21
dǎ wǎngqiú	打網球	打网球	20
dǎzhé	打折	打折	21
dǎzhēn	打針	打针	16
dàbáicài	大白菜	大白菜	37
dàduōshù	大多數	大多数	30
dàgài	大概	大概	9
dàgēdà	大哥大	大哥大	41
dāi (yì) huǐ(r)	待（一）會兒	待（一）会儿	5
dàifu	大夫	大夫	30
dàijià	代價	代价	38
dài	帶	带	28, 44
dàizi	帶子	带子	9
dài	袋	袋	30
dāndú	單獨	单独	17
dānwèi	單位	单位	17
dàngāo	蛋糕	蛋糕	15
dāng	當	当	2
dàochù	到處	到处	22
dào...wéizhǐ	到…爲止	到…为止	40
dào	倒	倒	16
dàobié	道別	道别	23

dé	得	得	16
dēng	燈	灯	36
dēnglóng	燈籠	灯笼	25
děngyíxià	等一下	等一下	5
děngyìhuǐ(r)	等一會兒	等一会儿	5
dìdao	地道	地道	32
dìdiǎn	地點	地点	18
dì(lǐ)xué	地（理）學	地（理）学	1
diǎnxíng	典型	典型	35
diànchē	電車	电车	11
diànnǎo	電腦	电脑	13
diàntī	電梯	电梯	32
diànyǐngyuàn	電影院	电影院	14
diànzǐyóujiàn	電子郵件	电子邮件	23
diāo	雕	雕	36
diào	掉	掉	21
diàochá	調查	调查	42
diē	爹	爹	38
dìng	訂	订	15
dōng	東	东	1
dōngtiān	冬天	冬天	10
dòngwùyuán	動物園	动物园	26
dòufǔ	豆腐	豆腐	37
dòu(fǔ)gān	豆（腐）乾	豆（腐）干	37
dú	讀	读	13
dúzhě	讀者	读者	33

dúchàng	獨唱	独唱	45
duǎn	短	短	13
duǎnzhàn	短暫	短暂	11
duì	對	对	26, 44
duìbùqǐ	對不起	对不起	27
duìmiàn	對面	对面	1
dùn	燉	炖	29
duōyīnzì	多音字	多音字	17
duōyú	多餘	多余	44
duōyún	多雲	多云	10

E

| érqiě | 而且 | 而且 | 21 |
| ěrduo | 耳朵 | 耳朵 | 38 |

F

fāshāo	發燒	发烧	16
fānqié	番茄	番茄	24
fǎn	反	反	27
fǎnyìng	反映	反映	45
fǎnzhèng	反正	反正	16
fàn cuòwù	犯錯誤	犯错误	37
fànhé	飯盒	饭盒	32
fāngfǎ	方法	方法	11
fāngshì	方式	方式	40
fángdōng	房東	房东	18
fángzū	房租	房租	18

fàngsōng	放鬆	放松	33
fēicháng	非常	非常	2
fēijī	飛機	飞机	11
fēnxī	分析	分析	45
fèndòu	奮鬥	奋斗	41
fēngwèi	風味	风味	12
fūfù	夫婦	夫妇	17
fú	扶	扶	38
fúhé	符合	符合	45
fúwù	服務	服务	27
fúzhuāng	服裝	服装	9
fù	賦	赋	40
fùzá	複雜	复杂	20
fùzhàng	付帳	付帐	14

G

gǎi	改	改	8
gài fángzi	蓋房子	盖房子	22
gàizhāng	蓋章	盖章	44
gān	乾	干	29
gānjìng	乾淨	干净	22
gānzào	乾燥	干燥	10
gǎn	趕	赶	30
gǎnjué	感覺	感觉	7
gǎnmào	感冒	感冒	16
gǎnxiè	感謝	感谢	3
gǎnlǎnqiú	橄欖球	橄榄球	20

gǎnpí	擀皮	擀皮	37
gǎnshòu	感受	感受	35
gāoáng	高昂	高昂	45
gāolóu	高樓	高楼	22
gāosùgōnglù	高速公路	高速公路	11
gǎo	搞	搞	27
gē	擱	搁	29
gēcí	歌詞	歌词	45
gēshǒu	歌手	歌手	45
gè	各	各	36
gè	個	个	36
gèdì	各地	各地	36
gèrénzhǔyì	個人主義	个人主义	44
gēnběn	根本	根本	7, 36, 44
gēnyuán	根源	根源	39
gōnggòngqìchē	公共汽車	公共汽车	11
gōnglù	公路	公路	11
gōnglì	功力	功力	35
gòngchǎnzhǔyì	共產主義	共产主义	44
gòngxiǎng	共享	共享	44
gòuwùzhōngxīn	購物中心	购物中心	14
gūdān	孤單	孤单	41
gǔdiǎnwénxué	古典文學	古典文学	40
gǔlì	鼓勵	鼓励	44
guāfēng	颳風	刮风	10
guà	掛	挂	25

guàibudé	怪不得	怪不得	2
guāndiǎn	觀點	观点	40
guàn	罐	罐	24
guànshū	灌輸	灌输	43
guànxǐshì	盥洗室	盥洗室	28
guāngmíng	光明	光明	39
guīzé	規則	规则	33
guójì	國際	国际	19
guójìzhǔyì	國際主義	国际主义	44
guójiā	國家	国家	12
guǒzhī	果汁	果汁	5

H

hǎixiā	海蝦	海虾	24
hánjià	寒假	寒假	11
háofù	豪富	豪富	41
hǎobuliǎo	好不了	好不了	16
hǎo jǐ tiān	好幾天	好几天	16
héshì	合適	合适	18
héfàn	盒飯	盒饭	32
hézi	盒子	盒子	19
hèn	恨	恨	22
hōng	哄	哄	38
hōngdòng	轟動	轰动	41
hónglǜdēng	紅綠燈	红绿灯	14
hòu	後	后	1
hòulái	後來	后来	4

hú	湖	湖	1
huáqiáo	華僑	华侨	8
huáyì	華裔	华裔	8
huáxuě	滑雪	滑雪	20
huàxué	化學	化学	1
huáijiù	懷舊	怀旧	45
huáiyí	懷疑	怀疑	45
huānlè	歡樂	欢乐	41
huānyíng guānglín	歡迎光臨	欢迎光临	14
huàn	換	换	18
huànqián	換錢	换钱	23
huāng	慌	慌	31
huí	回	回	27
huódòng	活動	活动	4
huópō	活潑	活泼	35
huóyuè	活躍	活跃	35
huǒchē	火車	火车	11
huòmiàn	和麵	和面	37
hùzhào	護照	护照	23

I

J

jīdàn	雞蛋	鸡蛋	24
jītuǐ	雞腿	鸡腿	24
jīhū	幾乎	几乎	30
jīliè	激烈	激烈	42

jiǎozi	餃子	饺子	37
jiǎozi pí	餃子皮	饺子皮	37
jiàoshì	教室	教室	1
jiàoyù	教育	教育	44
jiàoyùchéngdù	教育程度	教育程度	27
jiē	接	接	11
jiēshí	結實	结实	34
jiēzhe+verb	verb	verb	36
jiémùzhǔchírén	節目主持人	节目主持人	42
jīn	斤	斤	24
jǐn	緊	紧	37
jìnbù	進步	进步	7
jīngcháng	經常	经常	14
jīnglì chōngfèn	精力充分	精力充分	33
jīngxǐ	驚喜	惊喜	35
jiǔcài	韮（韭）菜	韭菜	37
jiùshìshuō	就是說	就是说	2
júhuā	菊花	菊花	24, 29
jùtǐ	具體	具体	39
juéduì bù/méi	絕對不沒	绝对不没	9

К

kāfēi	咖啡	咖啡	5
kāishuǐ	開水	开水	5
kāixīn	開心	开心	16
kàn bàozhǐ	看報紙	看报纸	7
kàn diànshì	看電視	看电视	7

kàn zhàopiàn	看照片	看照片	7
kǎoshì juànzi	（考試）卷子	（考试）卷子	43
kēzé	苛責	苛责	44
késòu	咳嗽	咳嗽	16
kě+verb	可	可	40
kěguān de shùmù	可觀的數目	可观的数目	40
kělè	可樂	可乐	5
kèchéng	課程	课程	34
kètīng	客廳	客厅	18
kěndìng	肯定	肯定	9
kōngqìwūrǎn	空氣污染	空气污染	23
kōngxū	空虛	空虚	41
kǒngjù	恐懼	恐惧	41
kǒngpà	恐怕	恐怕	11
kǔ	苦	苦	12
kùzi	褲子	裤子	9
kuàizi	筷子	筷子	24
kùn	睏	困	38

L

là	辣	辣	12
láojià	勞駕	劳驾	28
lǎobǎn	老闆（板）	老板	14
lǎorén	老人	老人	15
lǎorénjiā	老人家	老人家	32
lèyú	樂於	乐于	35
lèi	累	累	6

lèi	類	类	27
lèisì	類似	类似	35
lěng	冷	冷	10
lěngdàn	冷淡	冷淡	41
lěngqì	冷氣	冷气	16
lǐfà(fǎ)diàn	理髮店	理发店	27
lǐlùn	理論	理沦	40
lǐjiě	理解	理解	2
lǐwù	禮物	礼物	15
lián…dōu/yě	連…都也	连…都也	18
liánluò	聯絡	联络	23
liánxì	聯繫	联系	23
liàn jiànshù	練劍術	练剑术	20
liàn tàijíquán	練太極拳	练太极拳	20
liángkuài	涼快	谅快	10
liàngcí	量詞	量词	17
liáotiān(r)	聊天（兒）	聊天（儿）	5
liǎobùqǐ	了不起	了不起	34
lǐngdài	領帶	领带	9
liūbīng	溜冰	溜冰	20
liú	留	留	17
liúxuéshēng	留學生	留学生	12
liúxíng	流行	流行	5
liúxuě	流血	流血	31
lóng	龍	龙	15
lóu	樓	楼	1

luàn	亂	乱	13
lúnyǐ	輪椅	轮椅	42
lùnwén	論文	论文	30, 40
lǚxíngtuán	旅行團	旅行团	32
lǚyóu	旅遊	旅游	21
lùxù	陸續	陆续	43
lùlùxùxù de	陸陸續續地	陆陆续续地	43

M

máfan(fán)	麻煩	麻烦	11, 28
mǎkèsīzhǔyì	馬克思主義	马克思主义	44
mǎlù	馬路	马路	14
màibó	脈搏	脉搏	30
mǎntóudàhàn	滿頭大汗	满头大汗	20
máodùn	矛盾	矛盾	41
máoyī	毛衣	毛衣	9
màozi	帽子	帽子	9
méiguīhuā	玫瑰花	玫瑰花	24
méimáo	眉毛	眉毛	38
méi guānxi	沒關係	没关系	27
méi shì(r)	沒事儿	没事儿	13
méiyǒu shénme le	沒有什麼了	没有什么了	3
měi…dōu…	每…都…	每…都…	12
měiróngyuàn	美國人	美国人	27
měishì zúqiú	美式足球	美式足球	20
mēn, mèn	悶	闷	10
ménkǒu	門口	门口	25

mí	迷	迷	26
mílù	迷路	迷路	26
mǐ	米	米	26
miànbāo	麵	面	24
miàn(tiáo)	麵條	面条	15
miào	妙	妙	41
mínzúzhǔyì	民族主義	民族主义	44
mǐn'gǎn	敏感	敏感	39
míngxìnpiàn	明信片	明信片	19
mógū(dōnggū)	蘑菇（冬菇）	蘑菇（冬菇）	37
mótuōchē	摩托車	摩托车	11
mòshēng	陌生	陌生	41
mǔyǔ	母語	母语	2

N

náshǒucài	拿手菜	拿手菜	29
nǎlǐ nǎlǐ	哪裏哪裏	哪里那里	3
nà jiù suànle	那就算了	那就算了	28
nà yě kěyǐ	那也可以	那也可以	3
nán	南	南	1
nánzhuāng	男裝	男装	9
nǎodài téng	腦袋疼	脑袋疼	30
nǐ gànmá ne	你幹嘛呢	你干嘛呢	13
niàobù	尿布	尿布	38
niúnǎi	牛奶	牛奶	5, 24
niúròu	牛肉	牛肉	24
nóngmín	農民	农民	24

nǚ gāoyīn	女高音	女高音	45
nǚquánzhǔyì	女權主義	女权主义	44
nǚzhuāng	女裝	女装	9

O

P

pāi zhàopiàn	拍照片	拍照片	6
páiduì	排隊	排队	27
páijià	牌價	牌价	24
pángbiān	旁邊	旁边	1
pǎobù	跑步	跑步	20
pàochá	泡	泡	29
pào(kāi)	泡（開）	泡（开）	29
pàoshēng	炮聲	炮声	45
péi	陪	陪	27
píjiǔ	啤酒	啤酒	5, 24
píláo	疲勞	疲劳	30
pínglùn	評論	评论	39
pínglùnjiā	評論家	评论家	39
pòpòlànlàn	破破爛爛	破破烂烂	41
pòyīnzì	破音字	破音字	17
pūchuáng	舖床	铺床	44
pǔtōng	普通	普通	29

Q

qīwàng	期望	期望	44
qíshí	其實	其实	16

qúnzi	裙子	裙子	9

R

rè	熱	热	10
rècháo	熱潮	热潮	45
rènào	熱鬧	热闹	36
rónghé	融合	融合	44
róngxìng	榮幸	荣幸	39
rúcǐ	如此	如此	34
rúguǒ…dehuà	如果…的話	如果…的话	11
rúhé	如何	如何	43

S

sāichē	塞車	塞车	22
shāngchǎng	商場	商场	15
shāngliang	商量	商量	28
shàng	上	上	1
shàngxià	上下	上下	30
shàng xué	上學	上学	8
shǎnkāi	閃（開）	闪（开）	31
shāowēi	稍微	稍微	24
shétou	舌頭	舌头	30
shèhuìzhǔyì	社會主義	社会主义	44
shèshī	設施	设施	32, 42
shēn	伸	伸	30
shēngāo	身高	身高	38
shēntǐ	身體	身体	2

shénmede	什麼的	什么的	7
shènzhì	甚至	甚至	45
shēngcài	生菜	生菜	24
shēngchéng	生成	生成	43
shēnghuó	生活	生活	5
shēngwù(xué)	生物（學）	生物（学）	1
shěng	省	省	19
shī	詩	诗	40
shīfu	師傅	师傅	12
shīqù zhījué	失去知覺	失去知觉	31
shīzi	獅子	狮子	26
shíjìshàng	實際上	实际上	13
shítou	石頭	石头	26
shízìlùkǒu	十字路口	十字路口	14
shìjì	事蹟	事迹	45
shìyàn	試驗	试验	35
shǒutào	手套	手套	20
shǒuxiān	首先	首先	29
shōu	收	收	19
shōujù	收據	收据	14
shòu	瘦	瘦	16
shòudào	受到	受到	2
shòushāng	受傷	受伤	31
shūfu	舒服	舒服	10
shūjià	書架	书架	13
shūmíng	書名	书名	13

shūqíng	抒情	抒情	45
shú(shóu)xi	熟悉	熟悉	12
shǔjià	暑假	暑假	11
shù	束	束	24
shuǐ	水	水	5
shuǐdiànfèi	水電費	水电费	18
shuìmián	睡眠	睡眠	30
shūo(shuì)fúlì	說服力	说服力	35
shuōlái jiù cháng	說來就長	说来就长	17
shuòshì(xuéwèi)	碩士（學位）	硕士（学位）	34, 40
sījī	司機	司机	31
sīwéi	思維	思维	35
sòng	送	送	11
suān	酸	酸	12
suì	碎	碎	31
suǒyǐ shuō	所以說	所以说	37

T

tàidù	態度	态度	40
tāngchí	湯匙	汤匙	37
tǎng	躺	躺	16
tǎo rén xǐhuān	討人喜歡	讨人喜欢	38
tèbié	特別	特别	16
tèjià	特價	特价	5
tī zúqiú	踢足球	踢足球	20
tíqián	提前	提前	11
tíxǐng	提醒	提醒	16

tǐyùguǎn	體育館	体育馆	1
tǐwēn	體溫	体温	30
tǐzhòng	體重	体重	38
tián	甜	甜	12
tián	填	填	27
tiánbiǎo	填表	填表	27
tiāo	挑	挑	9
tiáoxiàn	調餡	调馅	37
tiē	貼	贴	19
tīng guǎngbō	聽廣播	听广播	7
tǐng hǎo	挺好	挺好	3
tōng	通	通	34
tōngdào	通道	通道	42
tóngyàng	同樣	同样	44
tóufa	頭髮	头发	17, 27
tóu téng	頭疼	头疼	30
tūrán	突然	突然	31, 32
tǔshēng tǔzhǎng	土生土長	土生土长	44
tuìxiū	退休	退休	2
tuō	拖	拖	16
tuōérsuǒ	托兒所	托儿所	43

W

wàzi	襪子	袜子	9
wàitào	外套	外套	9
wán(r)	玩（兒）	玩（儿）	4
wēixiǎn	危險	危险	11

wèi	餵	喂	38
wèi	爲	为	44
wèidào	味道	味道	12
wèikǒu	胃口	胃口	30
wèimíng	未名	未名	1
wénjiàn	文件	文件	23
wénshǐ	文史	文史	1
wényánwén	文言文	文言文	40
wòshì	臥室	卧室	18
wūrǎn	污染	污染	22
wúfǎ	無法	无法	35
wúzhèngfǔzhǔyì	無政府主義	无政府主义	44

X

xī	西	西	1
xīhóngshì	西紅柿	西红柿	24
xīzhuāng	西裝	西装	9
xīshēng	犧牲	牺牲	45
xíguàn	習慣	习惯	5
xǐzǎojiān	洗澡間	洗澡间	18
xì	系	系	1
xià	下	下	1
xiàxuě	下雪	下雪	10
xiàyǔ	下雨	下雨	10
xiàtiān	夏天	夏天	10
xián	鹹	咸	12, 29
xiàn	限	限	27

xiànzhì	限制	限制	42
xiànchéng	現成	现成	37
xiànjīn	現金	现金	14
xiànxiàng	現象	现象	45
xiàndàiwénxué	現代文學	现代文学	40
xiàn(jìnqù)	陷（進去）	陷（进去）	31
xiāngdāng(yú)	相當（於）	相当（于）	42
xiāngfǎn	相反	相反	35
xiǎngxiàng	想像	想像	22
xiàng…guǎi	向…拐	向…拐	14
xiàng(…děngděng)	像（…等等）	象（…等等）	12
xiǎochī	小吃	小吃	36
xiǎodāo	小刀	小刀	14
xiǎopéngyǒu	小朋友	小朋友	15
xiǎoshí	小時	小时	25
xiàolǜ	效率	效率	33
xiàoyuán	校園	校园	14
xiélì	協力	协力	35
xiézi	鞋子	鞋子	9
xīnxiān	新鮮	新鲜	29
xìnfēng	信封	信封	19
xínglǐ	行李	行李	11
xíngwéi	行爲	行为	39
xìng	性	性	33
xìngbié	性別	性别	27
xìngkuī	幸虧	幸亏	31

xìngqù	興趣	兴趣	7
xiōngdì jiěmèi	兄弟姐妹	兄弟姐妹	2
xūzì	虛字	虚字	40
xuǎn	選	选	8
xuéwèi	學位	学位	34
xuézhě	學者	学者	33
xuětǒng	血統	血统	43
xúnzhǎo	尋找	寻找	39
xùnliàn	訓練	训练	33

Y

yājīn	押金	押金	18
yán	沿	沿	26
yángé	嚴格	严格	43
yánjǐn	嚴謹	严谨	35
yánzhòng	嚴重	严重	16
yǎnchàng	演唱	演唱	45
yǎnzòu	演奏	演奏	45
yǎnjīng	眼睛	眼睛	38
yǎnlèi	眼淚	眼泪	20
yāo	幺	幺	31
yáogǔnyuè	搖滾樂	摇滚乐	45
yáoyuǎn	遙遠	遥远	41
yǎozì	咬字	咬字	45
yào	藥	药	16
yàobù(rán)	要不（然）	要不（然）	12
yàoshì…dehuà	要是…的話	要是…的话	11

yěxǔ	也許	也许	9
yīsheng	醫生	医生	2
yīyuàn	醫院	医院	16
yímín	移民	移民	41
yíxiàng	一向	一向	45
yíxiàzi	一下子	一下子	16
yídìng	一定	一定	9
yítào	一套	一套	30
yǐshàng/xià	以上下	以上下	27
yǐ…wéiróng	以…爲榮	以…为荣	43
yìbān	一般	一般	30
yìhuǐ(r)	一會兒	一会儿	16
yìwài	意外	意外	39
yìxìng	異性	异性	39
yīn	陰	阴	10
yǐnqǐ	引起	引起	39
yìnxiàng	印象	印象	34
yìnxiàngzhǔyì	印象主義	印象主义	44
yīngér	嬰兒	婴儿	32
yòng	用	用	14
yóu	油	油	12
yóu	郵	邮	19
yóujiàn	郵件	邮件	19
yóupiào	郵票	邮票	19
yóulǎn	遊覽	游览	32
yóuqí(shì)	尤其（是）	尤其（是）	40

yóuyǒng	游泳	游泳	20
yǒuxiào	有效	有效	30
yǒu xiàoguǒ	有效果	有效果	30
yòuérsuǒ	幼兒所	幼儿所	43
yòuéryuán	幼兒園	幼儿园	43
yòuzhìyuán	幼稚園	幼稚园	43
yú	魚	鱼	24
yǔmáoqiú	羽毛球	羽毛球	33
yǔsǎn	雨傘	雨伞	9
yùgāng	浴缸	浴缸	28
yuánlái	原來	原来	4
yuánzhuō	圓桌	圆桌	44
yuànyì	願意	愿意	12
yuèláiyuè	越來越	越来越	7
yuèduì	樂隊	乐队	45
yuèqì	樂器	乐器	45
yùliào	預料	预料	39
yǔnxǔ	允許	允许	39
yùn	運	运	19

Z

zánmen	咱們	咱们	1
zāng	髒	脏	22
zěnme bàn	怎麼辦	怎么办	13
zěnme gǎo de	怎麼搞的	怎么搞的	27
zěnme huí shì(r)	怎麼回事兒	怎么回事儿	27
zhǎngwò	掌握	掌握	40

zhàng'ài	障礙	障碍	42
zhàngfu	丈夫	丈夫	17
zhāojí	著急	著急	7
zhāopái	招牌	招牌	14
zhàoxiàng	照相	照相	7
zhàoxiàngjī	照相機	照相机	7
zhéxué	哲學	哲学	1
zhě	者	者	33
zhème…hái…	這麼…還…	这么…还…	20
zhèyàng	這樣	这样	42
zhèyàngba	這樣吧	这样吧	28
zhēn búcuò	真不錯	真不错	27
zhēnzhèng	真正	真正	2
zhèng	正	正	26
zhèngcháng	正常	正常	30
zhènghǎo	正好	正好	1
zhèngqián	掙錢	挣钱	41
zhī	枝	枝	24
zhī	隻	只	24
zhīhòu	之後	之后	14
zhīhūzhěyě	之乎者也	之乎者也	40
zhīpiào	支票	支票	27
zhīyīn	知音	知音	35
zhíyè	職業	职业	27
zhǐjiào	指教	指教	30
zhìbuliǎo	治不了	治不了	16

zhìshǎo	至少	至少	19
zhìyuànjūn	志願軍	志愿军	45
zhǒng	種	种	12
zhònglì	重力	重力	35
zhōunián	週年	周年	17
zhǔtí	主題	主题	45
zhǔyào	主要	主要	2
zhǔyì	主義	主义	44
zhùyuàn	住院	住院	16
zhuān	專	专	42
zhuānyè	專業	专业	7, 33
zhuànqián	賺錢	赚钱	41
zhuāng	裝	装	19
zhuàng	撞	撞	31
zīběnzhǔyì	資本主義	资本主义	44
zìcóng	自從	自从	38
zìdòng	自動	自动	32
zìxíngchē	自行車	自行车	11
zìxìnxīn	自信心	自信心	44
zìzūnxīn	自尊心	自尊心	44
zōnghé	綜合	综合	43
zǒng(éryán)zhī	總（而言）之	总（而言）之	45
zǒu guòlái/qù	走過來去	走过来去	10
zūyuēqīxiàn	租約期限	租约期限	18
zuǐba	嘴巴	嘴巴	38
zuǒyòu	左右	左右	17, 30